Everything
CAT

What Kids Really Want to Know About Cats

by
Marty Crisp

SCHOLASTIC INC.

New York Toronto London Auckland Sydney
Mexico City New Delhi Hong Kong Buenos Aires

Edited by Ruth Strother
Cover and text design by Michele Lanci-Altomare

ISBN 0-439-66411-X

15 14 13 12 11   10 11 12 13 14/0

Printed in the U.S.A.   40

First Scholastic printing, November 2004

The cats in this book are referred to as *he* or *she* in alternating chapters.

All photographs provided by Getty Images,
except for page 35, copyright © 2003 Michele Lanci-Altomare,
and page 46, copyright © 2003 Wendy Lutge.

Acknowledgments

SPECIAL THANKS TO PAUL J. CAPPIELLO, DVM, Peaceable Kingdom Animal Hospital, Ephrata, PA, and Julie Adams, DVM, Conestoga Animal Hospital, Hinkletown, PA, for their help in reviewing the manuscript. Please note that any errors are the author's alone.

Additional thanks to my editor, Ruth Strother, who really knows her stuff, and to NorthWord's Aimee Jackson, who changed publishing houses but didn't leave me behind. Here's to book five together, Aimee!

Dedication

IN MEMORIAM: ROBERTO J. VIANO, SEPTEMBER 20, 1944–September 20, 2002, a man who liked cats and loved his family.

—*M. C.*

contents

introduction • 7

Did cats come from dinosaurs? 8

How many breeds of cat exist today? 10

Did curiosity really kill the cat? 12

My cat doesn't come when I call her. Does she know her name? 14

Can you teach a cat tricks? 16

How much sleep does a cat need? 18

Why do cats purr? 19

Do cats communicate? 20

Why do cats play with their food? 22

Why does my cat stare at me? 24

Why did my cat bring me a bird he just killed? 25

How old can a cat live to be? 26

Why did our old cat disappear forever? 27

Why does my cat like catnip? 29

Why do my cat's eyes seem to glow in photographs? 30

Why do cats seem to have a hard time getting along? **31**

Why is my cat so picky about what he eats? **32**

Why does my cat lick herself? **34**

Why do cats eat grass? **35**

Should we have our cat declawed? **36**

How come my cat is afraid to climb down trees? **38**

Do cats always land on their feet? **40**

Why do cats hate water? **42**

Do cats really have nine lives? **44**

Why do cats like getting on top of the fridge? **46**

Why is a cat's tongue rough? **48**

Are there any famous cats? **50**

Why are so many people allergic to cats? **52**

Is a black cat bad luck? **54**

Do cats like people or don't they? **56**

strange cat facts • 59

resources • 62

Pedigreed or not, cats make wonderful friends and companions.

introduction

A CAT BY ANY OTHER NAME IS STILL A CAT.
In Chinese, it's *mio;* in Italian, it's *gatto;* and in Dutch, it's *poes;* but it all boils down to the same aloof yet curious creature we call "cat." Breeders have tried to create new shapes and sizes of cats, but the cat has always remained pretty much the same—cat-shaped. Many cat lovers believe this is because the cat is perfect and simply can't be improved.

The idea for this book started with dogs. I visit schools and since I'm an author of middle grade fiction about dogs, kids ask me questions about dogs. I collected those questions and answered them in my book called *Everything Dog: What Kids Really Want to Know About Dogs.* But in every school I visited, there were plenty of kids who didn't have dogs—they had cats. And those kids asked questions about cats. So I started trying to find the answers to kids' curious questions about nature's most curious animal, *Felis cattus* (formerly known as *Felis domesticus*).

Cats are important to the whole history of human civilization, so let's start at the beginning.

Did cats come from dinosaurs?

When the dinosaurs became extinct, many smaller fur-bearing creatures managed to hang on and evolve, or change, into animals we know today. A small, furry weasel-like creature with good teeth called the miacid was living 55 million years ago. This was the carnivore, or meat eater, who eventually evolved into the animal with the most impressive teeth ever seen on earth—the saber-toothed tiger.

Smilodons, which is scientific speak for saber-toothed tigers, used their 8-inch-long front teeth to stab their prey. Of course, saber-toothed tigers had to eat what they caught, and those huge front teeth look like they'd get in the way. A human's jaws can open to a 45 degree angle, maximum. But saber-toothed tigers had hinged jaws that opened up to a 90 degree angle, which allowed any kind of prey past their enormous front teeth.

Smilodons were the dominant cat on earth for millions of years. But this branch of the cat family turned out to be a dead end. It was another, less toothy, branch, called *Felis lunensis,* that led to modern cats. About 12 million years ago, these smaller, more adaptable catlike creatures were the start of the Felidae, or cat, family. They evolved into two distinct varieties: *Panthera,* the big cats, who can roar because they have a small, movable bone at the base of their tongue, and *Felis,* the smaller cats, who cannot roar. (A third member of the cat family, *Acinonyx,* or cheetah, evolved from a different branch.) We're here to talk about *Felis cattus,* the most people-friendly member of the Felidae family.

About 4,500 years ago, cats got together with the ancient Egyptians. This early civilization stored grain, which attracted rats and mice. In turn, the rats and mice attracted cats. Those cats became the ancestors of all domestic cats today.

How many breeds of cat exist today?

As with dogs, different organizations in different countries (and sometimes in the same country) recognize different cat breeds. All over the world, somewhere between 80 and 100 pedigree breeds are now recognized. It's hard to pin down the exact number, since there always seems to be experimental breeds that have yet to achieve any group's official recognition. A few current unrecognized breeds are the Chinese harlequin, the palomino, the Mandarin, and the poodle cat.

The first cat show was held at the Crystal Palace, in London, England, in 1871. At that time, 25 different breeds participated. About 60 new breeds have developed since then in a little over 100 years. Cat breeds today include the glamorous Persian, the elegant Angora, the plush Russian blue, the round-eyed Burmese, and the slant-eyed Siamese. Cats can be big like the Maine coon, little like the Singapura, short-legged like the munchkin, long-legged like the Korat, tailless like the Manx, bushy-tailed like the Norwegian forest cat, hairless like the sphynx, thick-haired like the chinchilla Persian, curly-haired like the LaPerm, tufted-toed like the Somali, curly-eared like the American curl, or drop-eared like the Scottish fold. Some of the newer breeds, such as the Bengal, even have actual wild cat ancestry, bred from the wild Asian leopard cat to look like a spotted cheetah.

With cats, however, far more than with dogs, mixed breed cats (called random breds by cat breeders) far outnumber their purebred brothers and sisters. Of the whole domestic cat population, 2 percent are purebred. All the rest are mixed.

The Persian (opposite left) and the Siamese (opposite right) are 2 of the 100 or so breeds of cat.

Did curiosity really kill the cat?

Cats like to explore. And they learn quickly. They're instinctively cautious when they approach new things, but they're also ready to figure out whatever needs figuring: opening a latch, nabbing a bologna sandwich off the kitchen counter, or avoiding a toddler who pulls tails. A curious cat once survived 37 days inside a vending machine when she slipped through the food slot. A small kitten examining the end of a vacuum cleaner was accidentally sucked into the hose and survived. Curiosity does not always kill the cat, but it does give him some close calls.

Cats are known for their curiosity.

My cat doesn't come when I call her. Does she know her name?

Your cat definitely hears you. A cat's ears have pinnae, or ear cones, that turn in all directions like radar. We can't move our ears at all (okay, most of us can't). But a cat's pinna has more than 20 muscles working to allow it to turn and pick up sound coming from all sides, including from behind. A cat usually sits still to listen because it's harder to pinpoint sounds when on the move.

Humans can hear sound up to 20,000 megahertz (a measurement of sound). Dogs can hear 35,000 to 40,000 megahertz. Cats pick up an astonishing 100,000 megahertz. They can even hear the ultrasonic sounds that are known to precede natural occurrences such as earthquakes, volcanic eruptions, and electrical storms.

Chances are good that your cat knows her name, too. And when she believes she has something to gain, she'll come when called. Although she hears you call, she's asking the question that has helped cats survive for thousands of years: What's in it for me?

A cat's ears are made to pick up sounds from all around.

Can you teach a cat tricks?

The lion and tiger tamers in the circus think you can. And think about the useful things house cats learn to do and continue to do without coaching. They use a litter pan, meow to be let out, and frequently learn to open doors. They also seek out high vantage points, sometimes balancing on impossibly small objects just to get to where they want to be. Pretty talented, these cats!

Cats can learn tricks— especially if there is something in it for them!

How much sleep does a cat need?

It seems like cats are always sleeping. And it's true that left on their own cats sleep away as much as 75 percent of any given day. That's 18 hours a day. Cats with active companions tend to stay awake more, enjoying the interaction. But remember, cats are predators in the wild, always on the lookout for their next meal. Much of the time, scientists have learned, cats sleep lightly, waking as often as every several minutes. Even in sleep, they are alert to what's around them. This is where the term *catnap* comes from. Only about 30 percent of a cat's sleeping time is spent in the kind of deep sleep human beings try to achieve when we go to bed at night.

Catnapping is a favorite "activity" among cats.

Why do cats purr?

Purring can definitely signal contentment. But that's not the only reason cats purr. They may purr to invite play, to soothe a threatening enemy, or to reassure other cats that they mean no harm.

Experts disagree quite a bit over how a cat purrs. Some think a purr is the sound of turbulence in the main vein of a cat's heart. Others think that when a cat arches his back, the blood vibrates through his body, resonating in his sinuses and producing the sound we call a purr. Most scientists, however, think the purr is the sound of a vibrating membrane called the false vocal cord, located close to the cat's actual vocal chords.

Do cats communicate?

Some people believe cats can talk, although we haven't translated cat-speak to date. They meow to signal a need for attention or food. They gurgle (a high-pitched, friendly greeting), chat (a soft meow), screech (when they're upset), caterwaul (usually a tomcat's territorial challenge to other cats), hiss (a warning), growl (a threat), snarl (a bigger threat), or click their teeth as if chattering with cold (they want their prey, or food, so badly that their mouths are already working on chewing it).

Cats also say a lot with body language. They arch their backs and raise their fur as a threat or warning and an effort to look larger. They also crouch in readiness for whatever's coming. They move their ears: forward (friendly interest), slightly back (defensiveness), and flattened (fear). Their tails are telling, too: rapid side-to-side tail movements, a bit like wagging (excitement); tail up, held still (friendly greeting); and tail up, slightly twitching (alertness, possibly

A cat can use body language and her voice to get her point across.

readying for an attack). The saying *pussyfooting around* comes from a cat's body language when preparing for a fight: approaching, backing off, coming back, and backing off again. Cats may seem silent and mysterious, but they have a lot to say to people who know how to look and listen.

Why do cats play with their food?

Cats in the wild hunt animals for food. They are good at catching rodents such as rats and mice by the tail. A creature held down only by its tail can still bite. Cats don't want to be injured by whatever they've got trapped under a paw, so a

cat "plays" with, or teases, the creature he's captured. He wants to tire it out to the point where he can easily lunge in for the kill without worrying about teeth, beaks, or claws fighting back. This instinctual behavior looks funny, however, when done with a piece of kibble.

Why does my cat stare at me?

Most of the time, she's not staring at you, she's staring through you. The fact is she's not really using her eyes at all. She's using a sixth sense. A cat uses her mouth to pull scent into a small tube just behind her upper front teeth. The tube attaches to the Jacobson's organ.

When a cat appears to be staring with her mouth just slightly open, she is using her Jacobson's organ to sample the air. This is called the flehmen response. The German word *flehmen* translates roughly into "grimacing," but the act looks more like a vacant staring into the distance, or, perhaps, at you. But she isn't. She is preoccupied with surrounding smells to which you don't have a clue. She is reading the *Odor News* in her territory.

Why did my cat bring me a bird he just killed?

He loves you. He really loves you. A cat considers dead or, sometimes, half-dead prey a "gift." A thank-you note would be nice, but it is not expected.

How old can a cat live to be?

A 1-year-old cat is considered to be equivalent to a 19- or 20-year-old person. After 1 year, the rough formula is 4 years of a human life equals 1 year of cat life. By that tally, cats are middle-aged when they're 8 to 10 and hit retirement age around 12 or 13. The majority of cats live to be from 9 to 15 years old, but a few cats have been documented living into their 30s. An American tabby cat named Puss, who lived from 1903 to 1939, died at the ripe old age of 36 and holds the record.

Some cats have lived into their 30s, but the average cat lives to be about 15 years old.

An old cat may feel
threatened by his illnesses.

Why did our old cat disappear forever?

A cat facing illness or death is aware only that he is being threatened. He cannot find the source of the threat, but the instinctual response is to hide. Unfortunately, you can't hide from death. Some old cats run off not because they want to die alone, but because they think they can outwit the ultimate predator (death) by sneaking away. Sometimes they do such a good job of hiding that their human family is left wondering what happened to them.

Some cats become addicted to catnip.

Why does my cat like catnip?

There are actually 250 varieties of catnip, or *Nepeta cataria,* all in the mint family. Catnip is an herb that contains a chemical called nepetalactone. It affects some cats the way chocolate affects some people. It causes a delicious ecstasy that makes them want more—and more. Just a nip of catnip can send those cats rolling, rubbing, and batting their paws at imaginary butterflies.

Some cats don't like catnip. Others can get addicted to it, ignoring their food in favor of catnip. Although catnip's not toxic to cats, "catnipism," like alcoholism, can be a hard habit to break.

Why do my cat's eyes seem to glow in photographs?

Cats' eyes are specially adapted, or made, for seeing at night, the time when most wild cats hunt. Every cat's eye contains a tapetum lucidum, a special membrane that reflects light not absorbed by the retina. (The retina is the innermost layer of the eye and is connected to the brain.) This reflecting quality gives the cat's retina a second chance to receive light, improving night vision greatly. The tapetum lucidum also reflects light back to the camera, making cats' eyes look as if they are glowing in photographs.

Why do cats seem to have a hard time getting along?

Cats aren't pack animals. They're solitary hunters, and they are territorial. But they're also sociable. If they have to share the same territory, cats organize themselves into a group, with a top cat and a next-to-the-top cat and so on. A territory can be as large as a square mile or as small as a square foot. Controlling land or a house (territory) is what puts a cat on top. But some areas in a territory, such as a couch or water bowl, are considered communal and are shared without complaint.

Cats are solitary animals, but they can learn to get along with others.

Why is my cat so picky about what he eats?

Some cats don't like to eat where there is a lot of activity. A cat dish in the middle of kitchen traffic could drive your cat away when you sound the dinner gong. And there's also the possibility that if your cat does any outside roaming, he is picking up snacks from other people, from garbage cans, or even catching something fresh. A cat may only nibble at his dinner because it's just too much food. One can of cat food equals about five mice.

A cat's sense of taste diminishes with age, making the cat seem more finicky than ever. Since a cat "tastes" smells, he prefers food that doesn't come straight from the fridge. Cold food isn't as smelly as food at room temperature. The fact is your cat isn't unreasonable. He only wants what he wants, when he wants it, where he wants it, and in the amount he wants. Who you calling picky?

*Your cat may
be a picky eater
because he's getting
between-meal snacks.*

Why does my cat lick herself?

Cats spend a third of their waking hours using their tongues to groom themselves. A cat has a barbed tongue that acts like a pick to get the knots out of fur. But grooming isn't just about looking good. It also removes dead hair and skin as well as leaves, mud, and parasites such as fleas and ticks. It tones muscles, stimulates blood circulation, and provides vitamin D (which is produced on the skin by exposure to sunlight). It helps control body temperature and relieves tension. In short, it feels good, which is every cat's goal.

Cats spend much of their waking hours grooming themselves.

Why do cats eat grass?

All that grooming means some fur gets swallowed. Natural mucus in a cat's body can cause this fur to clump together into a dark mass commonly called a hair ball. Eating grass helps a cat regurgitate, or vomit up, these hair balls before they can block the cat's digestive tract.

But the most important reason cats eat grass is for the folic acid in grass "juice." In the wild, cats get this vitamin from the vegetable matter in the stomach contents of the mice and moles they gulp down whole. But domestic cats, fed on canned meat or kibble diets, sometimes need more of this essential vitamin. Folic acid helps build healthy blood and gives a cat speed and stamina.

Should we have our cat declawed?

Although veterinarians remove the claws only from the front paws, most cat experts say declawing mutilates a cat for the comfort of human beings. The surgery has been outlawed in Great Britain and in many other countries.

A cat's claws can be protracted, or extended. But a cat does not have conscious control over the process by which her claws move in and out. When a cat stretches or flexes her paw, as when reaching for prey, ligaments attached to the claws automatically tighten. This tightening pushes the claws forward and outward.

A cat's claws are exposed when she stretches out her paw.

In a normal relaxed position, a domestic cat's claws are sheathed and out of sight. This keeps cats from wearing down their claws as they walk.

Kittens learn from our reactions that we don't like to be touched with claws. While it's true that a cat without claws cannot scratch you (or the furniture), claws are a cat's main defensive weapons and an essential part of a cat's anatomy. Even cats who are only partially declawed have a hard time climbing trees and cannot defend themselves in the outside world. From a cat or a cat lover's point of view, declawing is a bad idea.

How come my cat is afraid to climb down trees?

Your cat realizes that his claws are like Captain Hook's hooked hand in *Peter Pan*. They curve and point backwards, like hooks, making them great for clinging to things on the way up. But they're not so hot for hanging on when coming back down. Cats can climb quite high, then realize that they can't get back down by jumping. And they can't climb down backwards. A cat high up in a tree sometimes feels trapped. That's why you have to call your dad or the fire department or anybody with a ladder and a bit of patience to coax the frightened cat back to safety.

A treed cat might feel trapped because he can't climb down backwards.

Do cats always land on their feet?

Cats have a remarkable ability to land on their feet by using their tail as a counterbalance. As a cat falls, she swivels in midair so her paws are pointing toward the ground. The cat then stretches out all four paws and arches her back to absorb the force of the impact.

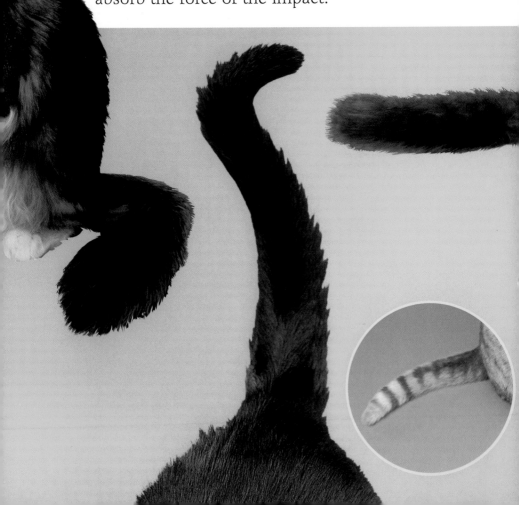

Cats use their tails while they fall to help them land on their feet.

There are countless stories of cats who've fallen amazing distances and have lived to tell about it. For instance, Gros Minou plunged an astounding 200 feet from the 20th floor of his master's Quebec penthouse, sustaining a fractured pelvis. He stayed far away from balconies after he recovered. There are also reports of cats being thrown from low-flying planes and surviving—but not without injury.

Even though a cat can right herself in the blink of an eye, a fall from a 2nd-story balcony could be tougher than a fall from a 4th-story balcony. A cat needs time to get her cushioned landing in place, and a 2nd-story fall may not allow for enough time.

Why do cats hate water?

You often see cats licking and licking themselves, trying to get every hair in just the right place. When a cat gets completely wet, the water soaks through both the outside coat and the undercoat. Try to imagine your cat licking himself dry and clean after a drenching. It can't be done. Or, at the very least, it will take hours—hours that could be better spent catnapping. A cat's coat also loses all insulating capacity when wet, and cats like to keep themselves at a stable temperature (normal feline body temperature is around 102.2 degrees). Not too hot. Not too cold.

Then there's the Turkish Van cat, the exception that proves the rule. An Angora cat from the desert region of Turkey's Lake Van, this cat loves swimming, especially if it's been raised near water. The Van has a unique coat with a cashmere-like texture that makes it water resistant. It also lacks an undercoat. When a Van goes in for a dip, he comes out relatively dry. In a desert region that regularly registers temperatures over 100 degrees Fahrenheit, swimming seems like the smartest thing a cat could do to stay cool.

It takes hours for a wet cat to dry off.

Do cats really have nine lives?

Maybe. Certainly, some cats have amazing survival stories. A Wisconsin cat named Joey was accidentally buried alive under 8 inches of concrete (proving it's not safe to be too curious when workers are pouring cement patios). Eleven days after disappearing, Joey clawed his way out of his concrete tomb, escaping with tiny nubs where his claws had been.

A California cat named Panda somehow clung to the luggage rack of a speeding car until his owner figured out why people were gesturing and yelling at her. After that experience, Panda found a new spot to sunbathe, staying away from car roofs. But Panda had nothing on Buttons, a British cat who accidentally took a 300-mile journey under the hood of a car. It wasn't until his owner stopped to check the oil that she found Buttons crouching behind the battery of the hot, smelly engine. That was a short jaunt compared to the stowaway cat who survived for over six weeks in a locked shipping container bringing a brand-new Mercedes-Benz from England to Australia.

1.

2.

4.

But no other cat can beat Oscar for survival. This tabby signed on as ship's cat on the German ship *Bismarck* in 1941. Ships and cats go together, right? There are a lot of rats and mice to catch onboard, and cats get respect from superstitious sailors who believe a ship's cat brings good luck. But luck wasn't with the *Bismarck* when it was sunk in battle and its crew became British prisoners of war. Oscar, on the other hand, made it to a life raft and was adopted by the crew of the British destroyer HMS *Cossack*. A short while later, when that ship was torpedoed, Oscar survived once again and found a new home on the British aircraft carrier HMS *Ark Royal*. It wasn't long before a German submarine in the Mediterranean Sea torpedoed the *Ark Royal*. Oscar was found hours later clinging to a plank. He spent the rest of his "nine lives" in a sailors' rest home in Ireland.

Scientifically speaking, cats have only one life just like the rest of us. But they seem to have a knack for survival.

5. **7.** **8.** **9.** **6.**

Why do cats like getting on top of the fridge?

Remember the song "Circle of Life" from the Disney movie *The Lion King?* The king addressed his subjects from atop a high bluff where he had a great view of everything around him. House cats are like our own little lion kings. They like to be at the highest point to survey their "king-doms." Kitchens are often the heart of a house, with a lot of action to monitor. Kitchen counters make good launching pads for reaching that spot atop the fridge where a cat can keep an eye on his territory.

Cats like to watch over
their territories from
high above.

Why is a cat's tongue rough?

The upper surface of a cat's tongue is covered with backward-pointing spines, or papillae. The papillae are used for combing fur and rasping big chunks of food into smaller bits. Cats also use their tongues for drinking water. The papillae give a cat's tongue more surface area, allowing her to pick up more water than if her tongue were smooth.

The cat's nimble tongue is to the cat what our hands and fingers are to us. Many experts believe cats consider being stroked by humans the same as being licked by another cat. It goes back to the old I-want-my-mommy behavior. Mother cat washed her kittens with her tongue. The kittens liked it because it made them feel loved and cared for. Petting brings on roughly the same feelings of kittenish pleasure and security.

A cat's rough tongue is used for combing fur, among other things.

Are there any famous cats?

The most famous cats, such as Garfield, Felix, and Tom of *Tom & Jerry,* come from cartoons. Literature gives us the dashing Puss in Boots, who saves his master from poverty and helps him get the girl, and, of course, Dr. Seuss's well-loved Cat in the Hat. There is also T. S. Eliot's famous 1939 book of poetry, *Old Possum's Book of Practical Cats,* on which the long-running Broadway musical *Cats!* was based.

When it comes to real-life cats, a lot of fame seems to come from advertising. Morris, a cat rescued from an animal shelter in Chicago, went on to become a household name as the spokes-cat for Nine Lives cat food. Likewise, S. H. III, a purebred chinchilla Persian, became famous as spokes-cat for Fancy Feast, supposedly the choice of picky (rich) cats. S. H.'s fame led him to parts in movies such as *National Lampoon's Christmas Vacation* and *Scrooged.*

Disney has made a whole pride of cat movies, including *The Aristocats, The Incredible Journey, The Three Lives of Thomasina, The Cat from Outer Space, Oliver & Company,* and *That Darn Cat.* Cats often play supporting roles in movies, too, sometimes as bad guys or just pets of bad guys (think *Austin Powers* and *Stuart Little*).

And cats have found fame as news makers at the start of the twenty-first century. Rainbow is the name of the first cloned cat, born December 22, 2001, at Genetic Savings & Clone (no kidding!), in Texas. In the fall of 2001, a mother cat and her three kittens were discovered curled up in a carton of napkins in the ruins of the World Trade Center. The rescued cat family became a symbol of hope to all the workers at Ground Zero. The mama cat was promptly named Hope, and her kittens were named Freedom, Amber, and Flag.

Why are so many people allergic to cats?

Cats have dander. So do dogs. So do you, but on you it's called dandruff. Cat dander is a mixture of shed hair, cat saliva, and tiny particles of shed skin. When dander floats in the air, it triggers an allergic response in some people. It makes them sneeze and cough, and some even feel itchy. It can become hard to breathe if your body's immune system overreacts to dander.

Cat dander is more potent than most other animal dander. Cats lick their fur, adding a protein from their saliva to the dander. Licking also helps release the dander into the air. This makes allergy-prone people more likely to react to cat dander than to dog or horse or people dander. And cat dander has remarkable staying power. It's been found in houses 10 years after a cat has moved out. Statistics show that one-third of cat owners are actually allergic to their cats. Former U.S. President Bill Clinton, for instance, was so allergic to his cat, Socks, that he had to have regular allergy shots so they could both live in the White House.

Is a black cat bad luck?

No way. In the Middle Ages, however, many superstitious people started to believe that cats of all colors—but especially black cats—were mixed up with devil worship and witchcraft. Widespread persecution of cats occurred all over Europe. Cats were shot, hung, and burned at the stake. But as the cat population shrank, the rat population grew. And rats carried the bubonic plague, a highly contagious disease that wiped out about one-third of the human population. It seems as though the cat got what he likes best—the last word.

strange cat facts

- The most complicated way of saying, "I love cats" is by calling yourself an ailurophile. The ancient Greek historian Herodotus first encountered cats in Egypt in the fifth century and called them *ailuroi,* meaning "tail wavers."

- The fattest cat on record was an Australian tabby who weighed just short of 47 pounds when he died at the age of 10 in 1986. He had a 33-inch waist.

- The smallest cat on record was a dwarf male blue point Himalayan, who was only 3 inches tall and 7 inches long when full grown.

- The richest cat ever was a feline named Blackie. His multimillionaire owner left over $15 million in his will to his 15 cats. Blackie survived the other 14 to become the single richest cat in the world.

- Cats were considered to be valuable mousers and ratters during the great California gold rush in the mid-nineteenth century. They were so valuable that miners paid $50 for a single mixed breed cat, which would be like paying about $1,000 for a cat today. Those miners' cats were worth their weight in gold!

• The worst musical instrument ever invented was the sixteenth century cat organ. It consisted of a dozen or so cats placed in open-front boxes with their tails poking out through holes in the back. The organ player either tugged on the tails, trying to make music with the resulting meows and hisses of protest, or used a keyboard with keys attached to spikes that prodded the poor cats. The instrument remained popular well into the seventeenth century.

• Cats have 30 teeth. That's 12 fewer than a dog and 2 fewer than a human.

• In the entire animal kingdom, only the cat, camel, and giraffe walk contralaterally. That means the right front leg moves forward at the same time as the left hind leg. Alternately, the left front leg moves forward with the right hind leg.

resources

BOOKS

ALDERTON, DAVID. *Eyewitness Handbook: Cats.* New York: DK Publishing, Inc., 1992.

BOYLAN, CLARE. *The Literary Companion to Cats.* London: Sinclair Stevenson Books, 1994.

COOPER, PAULETTE, AND PAUL NOBLE. *277 Secrets Your Cat Wants You To Know.* Berkeley: Ten Speed Press, 1997.

CUTTS, PADDY. *Cat Breeds of the World.* New York: Lorenz Books, 1999.

FOGLE, BRUCE, DVM. *The Encyclopedia of the Cat.* New York: DK Publishing, Inc., 1997.

FOX, DR. MICHAEL W. *Understanding Your Cat.* New York: Bantam Books, 1977.

Guinness Book of World Records 2001. New York: Bantam Books, 2000.

MORRIS, DESMOND. *Cat World.* New York: Penguin Books, 1997.

NASH, BRUCE, AND ALLAN ZULLO. *Amazing but True Cat Tales.* Compiled by Muriel MacFarland. Kansas City: Andrews and McMeel Publishing, 1993.

SCHNECK, MARCUS, AND JILL CARAVAN. *Cat Facts.* London: Quarto, Inc., 1990.

TABOR, ROGER. *Roger Tabor's Cat Behavior.* New York: Reader's Digest Books, 1997.

———. *Understanding Cats.* New York: Reader's Digest Books, 1997.

The Cat Fanciers' Association Cat Encyclopedia. New York: Simon & Schuster, 1993.

WEB SITES

www.5tigers.org/Directory/kids.html
Log onto this Web site for games, poems, kids' art, and tiger facts.

www.catclub.net
This Web site offers cat fun and information for all ages.

www.catoftheday.com
This Web site, presented by Pet Talk, features a new cat every day.

www.cattales.org/catpage.html
Visit wild cats from pumas to panthers.

www.cheetahspot.com
This Web site offers everything you ever wanted to know about the world's fastest cat.

www.claw.org/theater/
This Web site offers traditional tales told with cats in all the roles.

www.cynthialeitichsmith.com/kitlit.htm
Log onto this Web site, where an award-winning children's author recommends all the best kids' books about cats.

www.moscowcatmuseum.com/eng/cont.html
From Russia, this Web site gives us an English version of kids' pictures of cats, cat postcards, and funny cat stories.

www.nationalgeographic.com/cats/
Learn all about cats from this *National Geographic* Web site, Cats: Plan for Perfection.

www.nhm.org/cats/home.html
From the Natural History Museum of Los Angeles County comes the Web site based on the traveling exhibit *Cats! Wild to Mild*.

www.oldstylesiamese.com/kdpaws1.html
This Web site offers a kid-friendly primer on how cats—especially Siamese cats—operate.

www.tsimmes.com/cats/folklore/index.html
This Web site from the Folklore Society presents games, puzzles, folktales, poems, and interactive write-your-own stories featuring cats.

About the Author

AWARD-WINNING AUTHOR MARTY CRISP WRITES books for children and adults. She's also an animal lover and has worked for a veterinary clinic and an animal shelter. In addition to writing books, she is a journalist for the *Lancaster Sunday News* and has interviewed Newbery winner Phyllis Reynolds Naylor, literary legend John Updike, and has even covered concerts by performers such as Britney Spears and N'Sync. Ms. Crisp has four grown children and lives with her husband and their three dogs: Jessie, a Yorkshire terrier; Molly, a cairn terrier; and Sophie, a cavalier King Charles spaniel. If you'd like to know more about Marty Crisp, visit her Web site at **www.martycrisp.com.**

In Remembrance

Joseph Grasinski
MAY 24, 1895 - OCT. 6, 1962
Father

Lee Grasinski
NOV. 28, 1956 - JULY 7, 2008
Nephew

Genevieve Grasinski
SEPT. 28, 1925 - FEB. 22, 1962
Sister

Joseph Grasinski, Jr.
MAY 12, 1930 - OCT. 23, 1988
Brother

Shigeru Muraoka
AUG. 8, 1983 - DEC. 23, 2005
Nephew

Helen Grasinski
MAY 15, 1903 - MAY 20, 1990
Mother

Dale Hrouda
DEC 12, 1952 - JAN 24, 2004
Nephew

Dear Robert,

"The First time ever I saw your face" you were ascending the steps of St. Margaret Mary Church—Lemay, Detroit. I was greeted with "How may I help you?" Little did I realize that three years later I would be the one you chose to be your wife.

My life had been relatively simple ... from the little farm girl picking pickles and jumping in the hay stack to the peace, prayerfulness and service of the convent. It was you who had bought and built beautiful homes—the Hamilton House in Detroit, the Dunn Drive home on the Bay, and now, Chateau Chantal with the many spectacular views.

The nine months we lived in Europe will always remain deep in my heart. The trips and cruises to South America, the Mediterranean and Hong Kong were some of the most unforgettable times of my life.

Is there any greater joy than Marie-Chantal? In her own words, "Thank you, Dad, for your belief in me and your constant support. I love you."

Robert, I thank you for my most wonderful life ...

Undying Love,
Nadine

Library of Congress Cataloging-in-Publication Data
Begin, Nadine.
Feed My Lambs, Feed My Sheep : the Meals and Memories of a Lifetime/ by Nadine Begin

ISBN: 978-0-918293-05-3

Feed My Lambs
Feed My Sheep

The Meals and Memories of a Lifetime

BY **NADINE BEGIN**

When they had eaten, Jesus said to Simon Peter, "Simon son of John, do you love me more than these others do?" He answered, "Yes, Lord, you know I love you." Jesus said to him, "Feed my lambs." A second time he said to him, "Simon son of John, do you love me?" He replied, "Yes, Lord, you know I love you." Jesus said to him "Look after my sheep." Then he said to him a third time, "Simon son of John, do you love me?" Peter was hurt that he asked him a third time, "Do you love me? and said, "Lord, you know everything; you know I love you." Jesus said to him, "Feed my sheep." – JOHN 21:15

Welcome

The earth is full of the goodness of God. The seas are calm, the sun transforming a blanket of gray to a spectacular show of diamonds as the Crystal Serenity moves southward to Sicily.

The oceans are a compelling force. They speak to me of the power, majesty and wonderment of the Lord. His love is all encompassing; deep, wide and always present as this Mediterranean Ocean.

As I look over the veranda, this 93,500 square foot ship caresses the water resulting in yards and yards of beautiful Venetian lace.

This is a blessed time – twelve days to think about the many years of my life and recalling the beginning and the various twists and turns that have brought me here today.

Pilgrims
Beneath the shroud
Of the restless ocean,
The mighty whales
Heed the whisperings
Of creation,
Calling them to swim a journey
In honor of this sacred urging.
Hitching rides on flowing rivers,
Twisting, slapping
Breathing sky.
New moons
And full moons
And changing tides,
Clicking, whistling
Lullabies
To the cradle
Of their birth.
—EARLENE MCMILLIN

THIS PAGE: **Helen & Joseph Grasinski (Mommy & Daddy)**. OPPOSITE: **Valley Avenue, Grand Rapids, Michigan.**

1932-1950

FAMILY DAYS

Grand Rapids is a city located in the western part of Michigan and Valley Avenue is the street where I was born on January 15, 1932. Our house was stucco with a brick fireplace, an open back porch to shake out the piezena (feather bed). The front porch had a hole where we would watch for Daddy coming home from work.

I was baptized Patricia Marie in Sacred Heart Church and that was the beginning of a beautiful relationship with Jesus. We are still very close.

My heritage is Polish, German and Russian. My mother, Helen Fifelski, married Joseph Grasinski and was blessed with Carolyn, Genevieve, Frances, Joseph, Patricia, Angela and Mary. My mother was so beautiful— also prayerful, elegant, had a great sense of humor, loved beauty, music, and possessed a remarkable operatic voice.

Daddy was very loving, emotional and "easy" in the sense that we could always get anything we wanted from him. Daddy, as well as my mother, was a stylish dresser and was also gifted with an operatic voice. He was a lot of fun.

I was five years old when we moved to a farm near Wayland, Michigan. We didn't know it then but that was the happiest time of our life as a family. Despite the lack of basic conveniences (outhouse and Saturday night galvanized tub baths) we survived and lived happily.

Mother's Day Story

It was Mother's Day 1937. I had nothing to give my beautiful mother so I devised this plan: It was my job to walk to the neighboring farmer and buy milk. As I was walking, I thought, "I'll ask him if he'd like me to sing for him hoping that he'd give me some money." Well, that's exactly what I did and my plan worked!

Joe and I went to Wayland and bought a beautiful glass bowl. Mom, of course, loved it and kept it until she passed away on May 20, 1990. A little later, my oldest sister Carolyn came to visit on Mother's Day. She had the bowl in her hand and said to me, "Here's the bowl you sang for."

Remembering my Country Grandma

In My Garden
Amid the flowering iris stalks
And butterfly thrones
Of purple phlox
The gazing ball glittered
In the summer sun,
A mirror of silence
Reflecting the light
Of His kingdom come
To call and find me
Alone in my blue garden chair,
Listening to the humming, bumbling
Of bees at their task,
The flapping, splashing
Wings of birds at their bath,
Listening to a loving creator
Who illumines my soul
And guides my daily path.
–EARLENE MCMILLIN

There was always music in our home. All of us sang and most of us played an instrument. Gene played the piano and we'd sing for hours. I still remember many of the songs. Joe played the guitar. Country music was his specialty. Angel played the accordion. Our home exploded with music.

THIS PAGE: **Brother Joe**
OPPOSITE: **Baby Sister Mary**

THIS PAGE: **Patty.** OPPOSITE: **16th Street, Wayland, Michigan**

Faith played an important part: Sunday Mass, a rosary recited every day in May, morning and night prayers. We attended St. Stanislaus Church in Hilliards, sang in the choir, and were taught by the Felician Sisters in a Polish school.

I was in the 7th grade when Sister Mary DeChantal told us about the life of Saint Theresa. The more I heard about her the more I wanted to be just like her. I even tried sleeping on the floor like she did. The more I thought about it the more I desired to enter the convent and give my life completely to Christ. The seed was planted.

I attended Hopkins High School, a small public school. I chose to study home economics, dated, and wore a beautiful yellow gown to the prom. From the planting of the seed to the actual growth there were moments of extreme doubt. I loved so many things; pretty clothes, dancing, my family, and most especially my brother Joe.

Joe was a year and a half older and we shared a love of country music. He was an aspiring star and I was the official prayer-er. We spent many hours listening to the National Barn Dance and The Grand Ole Opry on the radio.

But above all there were quiet times in my life where, indeed, I felt the powerful presence of Jesus and His love for me. I knew I had to leave all and follow Him. "If anyone wishes to come after me, he must renounce himself, take up his cross and follow me, says the Lord." (Mt. 16:24)

I remember walking into our living room three times to say goodbye to my Daddy. Words were impossible. He was crying and so was I. My mother was sad but also happy that I was going to be a nun. Daddy said, "Patty, if you don't go I promise you anything, whatever you want."

On June 17, 1950 my brother took me to the train station. His eyes reflected sadness and encouragement. We both hugged and cried and off I went.

Love runs through our families,
Reaches hearts and lives,
Connecting distant members
Over miles and time through memories.
–INSPIRED BY MAYA ANGELOU

The Recipes

The recipes that follow reflect the harshness of the Depression and the simple life on the farm. We had a garden, a pickle patch, a pear tree, chickens, cows, horses and pigs. For beauty we had a tulip tree and for escaping there was an evergreen tree where we would climb to the top and hide. Is anything else really necessary? We were rich! We had a home, our entire family, food, love, music and laughter.

Carolyn, my oldest sister who still lives on the farm commented, "We ate very simply and it did not hurt us. Mom made the best pies ever — apple, mince meat, rhubarb and our favorite custard and coconut cream. Mom's pot roast, pork and beef cooked with carrots, onions, and potatoes could never be duplicated."

We frequently would go to the movies on Sunday and could hardly wait until we got home because we knew our favorite dish of chop suey would be waiting for us. I still enjoy eating chop suey on Sundays.

1932-1950
RECIPES

SOUPS & SALADS
Duck Soup *(Czarnina)*
Dumplings
Old Fashioned Tomato Bisque
Dill Pickle Soup
Cabbage Salad

MAIN DISHES
Chop Suey
Kielbasa
Baked Ham *(Szynka)*
Chili Con Carne
Baked Oysters
Cheese or Plum Dumplings *(Pierogi)*

VEGETABLES & SIDE DISHES
Cornmeal Mush
Potato Pancakes
Egg Pancakes
Cucumbers in Sour Cream
Wax Beans in Sweet-Sour Sauce
Dandelion Greens

BREAD, PASTRY, DESSERTS
White Bread
Plain Yellow Cake
Mom's Apple Pie and Glaze
Mom's Custard Pie
Bread Pudding
Mystery Cake of 1932
Vanilla Butter Frosting
Johnny Cake
Aunt Carolyn's Popcorn Balls
Mom's Coconut Cream Pie
Polish Bows (Chrusciki)
Mom's Special Tomato Preserves
Genevieve's Upside Down Cake

Genevieve's Pineapple Upside Down Cake
(RECIPE PG. 19)

Duck Soup (*Czarnina*)

This recipe can be made with molasses instead of duck's blood. Serve with dumplings.

½ duck, cut up 2-3 lbs.
1 qt. water
1 stalk celery
1 carrot
2 sprigs parsley
3 whole allspice
2 whole cloves
½ lb. dried pitted prunes
¾ cup molasses
2 T. flour
1 cup sour cream
1 qt. duck or goose blood
Salt, pepper, and lemon juice to taste

Cover duck with water in a large kettle. Add salt. Bring to a boil. Skim off foam. Place vegetables and spices into a cheesecloth bag and add to the soup. Cover and continue boiling for an hour.

Remove spice bag. Remove meat from kettle, debone, chop meat and return to the soup. Add dried fruit and cook for another 30 minutes. Blend sour cream and flour until smooth. Add blood or molasses a little at a time while beating. Add about 1 cup of the hot soup to the sour cream mixture and blend. Pour mixture into the soup. Bring soup to a boil stirring constantly. Add salt, pepper, and lemon juice (or vinegar) to taste. Serves 8 to 10.

Dumplings

4 cups flour
4 eggs
1 tsp. salt to taste
½ tsp. baking powder
Milk as needed to make stiff dough

Combine all ingredients. Mix. Using a tablespoon, dribble small bits of dough into boiling salted water. Cook 5 minutes and drain.

Old Fashioned Tomato Bisque

This is a Depression staple which is inexpensive, easy and tastes pretty good.—Carolyn

2 cups fresh tomatoes, peeled
½ tsp. baking soda
2 cups milk
1 T. butter
1 tsp. salt
½ tsp. pepper

Place tomatoes in a kettle and simmer until tender. Add baking soda. In another pan scald milk. (This is important so that the soup will not curdle.) Add tomatoes to milk and stir. Add butter, salt and pepper and a little sugar. Stir well.

Dill Pickle Soup

2 cups white wine
6 cups rich chicken stock, homemade preferred
2 carrots, grated
2 cups pared and cubed potatoes
1 cup thinly sliced celery
5 large Polish dill pickles, coarsely grated
½ cup milk
2 T. flour
1 egg
5 T. sour cream
Salt & pepper to taste
Finely chopped parsley or fresh dill
Vinegar (optional)

In a large pot, combine the stock, carrots, potatoes, and celery. Cook covered over low heat until the potatoes are soft, about 12 minutes. Add the pickles and cook for 15 minutes more. Combine the milk and flour and beat until smooth. Stir a small amount of the hot soup into flour mixture. Mix until smooth and return to soup, stirring well. Bring the soup to a boil, stirring frequently until the soup is slightly thick. Remove from heat.

Beat the egg with sour cream until smooth.

Pour a small amount of the hot soup into the sour cream mixture. Add to the soup and stir until smooth. Keep the soup warm but do not boil, or it will curdle. Add the salt and pepper to taste. Garnish with the dill or parsley. If you desire a soup that is sour, add about ¼ cup vinegar. Serves 8.

Cabbage Salad

1 tsp. salt
¼ tsp. pepper
2 T. sugar or honey
¼ cup chopped green pepper
½ tsp. dry mustard
1 tsp. celery seed
1 chopped apple or maraschino cherries
  or both
A sprinkle of Parmesan cheese and paprika
¼ cup chopped red pepper
2 T. finely chopped onion
4 cups finely shredded cabbage

DRESSING:
½ cup mayonnaise
½ cup sour cream
2 tsp. lemon juice or cider vinegar

In large bowl, place all ingredients in order listed. Mix well and add dressing. Sprinkle with Parmesan cheese and paprika.

Chop Suey

1 lb. pork cut into 1-inch cubes
1 lb. veal cut into 1-inch cubes
1 cup onion, diced
½ cup celery cut into chunks
3 T. molasses
8 T. soy sauce
Cooked rice
6 T. cornstarch
1 can bean sprouts and 1 can water chestnuts and reserve juice
½ cup brown sugar
1 cup fresh mushrooms
Salt & pepper to taste

Soak meat, molasses, salt & pepper, and soy sauce in pan for ½ hour. Add enough water to cover meat. Add celery and onions. Roast in oven 350º until meat is well done. When celery and onions are almost done, add bean sprouts and mushrooms. Add brown sugar. Take reserved juice from bean sprouts and water chestnuts. Add cornstarch. Use this as a thickener for chop suey. Simmer for 15 minutes and serve over rice.

Kielbasa and Horseradish with Red Beet Dip

1 ring kielbasa (approx. 2 lbs.)
4 oz. jar white horseradish, prepared
16 oz. can red beets, whole
2 T. sugar
2 T. vinegar, white
Salt and pepper to taste

Grate beets, mix with horseradish. Mix sugar and vinegar together and add to beet mixture. Salt, pepper to taste. Place *kielbasa* in pan and cover. Add ¾ cup water and heat in 350º oven for 45 minutes. Drain and cut into desired slices. Place *kielbasa* slices on a platter and use red beets with horseradish as dip.

Baked Ham (*Szynka*)

5 lbs. smoked ham, butt end
6 maraschino cherries
6 pineapple rings
1 tbs. prepared mustard
1 qt. ginger ale
1 cup brown sugar

Score ham and place pineapple rings, cherries on ham fastening with wooden picks. Put ham in a baking pan and pour ginger ale over it. Bake in 350º oven for two hours. Baste every ½ hour with the juice from the pan. Remove from oven. Make paste out of mustard and brown sugar; use pan juice to get a spread consistency. Spread on ham, raise temperature to 425º and bake for 15 minutes until browned.

Chili con Carne

I learned how to make chili in Home Economics classes.

2 lbs. ground beef
1 green pepper, chopped
2 T. olive oil
1 ½ tsp. salt
2 garlic cloves, minced
2 tsp. chili powder
2 medium onions, chopped
⅛ tsp. cayenne pepper
1 tsp. ground cumin
1 tsp. sugar
1 tsp. dried oregano
1 can (16 oz.) kidney beans, undrained
2 cans (16 oz. each) tomatoes with liquid,
  chopped

In a large kettle, brown ground beef. Drain and set aside. In the same kettle, heat oil; sauté garlic and onions over low heat until onions are tender. Stir in green pepper, cumin and oregano. Add tomatoes, beef, and kidney beans. Simmer for 20 minutes in medium heat until sauce is thickened.

NOTE: We had a country Grandma and a Wayland Grandma. It was Wayland Grandma Anna who taught me always to add a little sugar when using tomatoes. I like to use brown sugar instead of granulated sugar.

Baked Oysters

¾ cup all purpose flour
⅛ tsp. salt
⅛ tsp. pepper
⅔ cup grated Romano cheese
¼ cup minced fresh parsley
½ tsp. garlic salt
2 eggs, beaten
1 cup dry bread crumbs
2 T. olive oil
1 pint shucked oysters or 2 cans (8 oz.
  each) whole oysters, drained

In a shallow bowl, combine flour, salt and pepper. In another bowl, combine bread crumbs, Romano cheese, parsley and garlic salt. Coat oysters with flour mixture, dip in eggs, then coat with crumb mixture. Place in a greased 15-by-10-by-1 inch baking pan. Drizzle with oil. Bake at 400º for 15 minutes or until golden brown. Serve with tartar sauce.

Cheese or Plum Dumplings (Pierogi)

Make these ahead and keep on hand in refrigerator or freezer for quick lunches or suppers. Double recipe if desired.

3 cups flour
½ tsp. salt
1 egg, slightly beaten
Water
Cheese-onion filling or sugared plums
Boiling water
Butter or margarine
Sour cream

In bowl, combine flour and salt. Add egg and enough water to form a ball. Divide dough in half. On lightly floured surface, roll out each half about ⅟₁₆ inch thick. With small bowl or wide glass, cut out twelve 4-inch circles. Place about 1 generous tablespoon cheese-onions filling off center of each circle; fold dough over as for turnover and, with fingers, pinch edges together to seal firmly.

Cook a few at a time in kettle of boiling water just until *pierogi* float to top, about 1 to 2 minutes. At this point *pierogi* may be cooled, divided for desired servings, wrapped airtight in plastic bags and refrigerated or frozen. Will keep 4 to 5 days in refrigerator, up to 6 months in freezer.

To serve, fry quickly in small amount of butter over medium heat just until lightly browned. Serve with sour cream. Makes 24.

CHEESE-ONION FILLING:
In bowl, combine 1 lb. farmer or pot cheese, 1 small finely chopped onion, 2 eggs, dash each of salt and pepper; mix well.

SUGARED PLUM FILLING:
Cut 12 fresh, firm purple plums in half; remove pits and sprinkle with sugar. Use one plum (depending on size) per dumpling.

Cornmeal Mush

This was a stand-by served often in the Depression era.

¾ **cup cornmeal**
¾ **cup cold water**
2 ½ **cups boiling water**
¾ **tsp. salt**
2 T. **margarine or butter**
Flour

Mix cornmeal and cold water in saucepan. Stir in boiling water and salt. Cook, stirring constantly until mixture thickens and boils. Reduce heat. Cover and simmer; 10 minutes. Spread in greased loaf pan. Cover and refrigerate until firm. Invert pan on plate to unmold. Cut into one-inch slices. Heat margarine or butter in skillet. Coat slices in flour and cook on low heat until brown on both sides. Serve with maple-flavored syrup.—*Carolyn*

Potato Pancakes
4 eggs
6 medium potatoes
2 T. flour
1 onion
1 tsp. salt
¼ **tsp. pepper**
½ **tsp. baking powder**

Grate potatoes and onion. Place potatoes in cheesecloth and squeeze out excess liquid. Add baking powder, flour, salt and pepper. Add eggs. Heat frying pan with shortening. Drop potato mixture by tablespoons into hot shortening. Sauté both sides until crisp and brown. Serve with sour cream and applesauce.

Egg Pancakes
3 eggs
¾ **cup flour**
1 ¼ **cups milk**
Dash salt

Combine all ingredients. Pour a thin layer into hot skillet. Fry until set. Turn and brown lightly. Serve with boiled syrup made with sugar, water, and light corn syrup.

Cucumbers in Sour Cream
3 cups sliced cucumbers
Salt to taste
¼ **cup fresh dill or 2 T. dry dill weed**
1 cup dairy sour cream or yogurt

Sprinkle cucumbers with salt. Let stand for 30 minutes. Pat dry with paper towels. Stir dill into sour cream. Add cucumbers and mix well. Serves 4 to 6.

Wax Beans in Sweet Sour Sauce

1 ½ lbs. of fresh wax beans cut in one-inch
   squares
3 T. butter
3 T. flour
Vinegar
Sugar

Cook beans in salted water. Make a roux
with butter and flour. Add water from beans.
Blend. Add vinegar and sugar with beans to
taste. Combine with beans.

Dandelion Greens

*Wayland Grandma Ann would come and help
Mom and taught her many things. I remember
walking behind her as she went into the yard in
search of dandelion greens. She'd pick only those
that did not have a flower stem, as they were very
bitter.–Carolyn*

1 qt. dandelion greens
1 cup sour cream
1 egg
1 tsp. butter
2 tsp. sugar
1 T. vinegar

Wash greens carefully. Make a mixture of a
cup of sour cream, well-beaten egg, salt, butter and sugar dissolved in vinegar. Let come
to a boil. Add greens.

Sweet Caroline, 1946

White Bread

2 potatoes (medium size)
2 T. sugar
2 pkg. dry yeast
1 T. oleo or lard
2 tsp. salt
3 or 4 cups Robinhood or Pillsbury flour

Boil potatoes in 1 quart of water and mash.
In a large bowl place sugar, oleo, salt, and
water from potatoes and the mashed potatoes. Combine flour and yeast. Add slowly to
ingredients. Knead the dough. Place in a covered greased bowl and let rise. On a lightly-
floured board divide into two (2) parts.
Shape loaf, place in a greased pan (3x9). Let
rise. Bake 375º for 45 minutes. Good luck!
–Aunt Rose Iciek

Plain Yellow Cake

*Whenever Mom made this cake, we all gathered
around and watched her slice it. She would cut it
in the shape of a star. I was always hanging
around to pick up any coconut that fell on the
table. I always said, "When I grow up and get
rich, I will buy a whole pound of coconut."–
Carolyn*

2 cups all purpose flour
1 ½ cups sugar
3 ½ tsp. baking powder
1 tsp. salt
½ cup shortening (margarine)
1 cup milk
1 tsp. vanilla
3 eggs

Have oven at 350º. Grease and flour two 8"
or 9" round layer pan. Beat all ingredients in
large mixer bowl on low speed for 30 seconds. Beat on high for 3 minutes. Bake layers
30-35 minutes. Frost with vanilla butter frosting. Sprinkle liberally with coconut.

Mom's Apple Pie and Glaze

2 ½ lbs. tart green cooking apples
1 cup granulated sugar
1 tsp. ground cinnamon
¼ tsp. salt
2 T. unsalted butter, cut into bits
1 T. lemon juice
3 T. all-purpose flour
½ tsp. freshly grated nutmeg
1 T. water or apple cider
Prepared double crust pastry

Position a rack in the center of the oven and preheat to 425º. On a lightly floured surface roll out ½ of the pastry to a 12" round. Fold in half or in quarters in order to transfer to a 9" pie pan. Unfold and ease the pastry into the pan without stretching. Refrigerate until the oven is preheated and the apple fie filling is prepared.

Peel the apples and quarter lengthwise. Core them and cut into wedges about ½" thick (about 7 cups). In a large bowl combine the sugar, flour, cinnamon, nutmeg, and salt; add the apples and toss well. Add the lemon juice and, if the mixture seems dry, add about a tablespoon of water or apple cider. Turn the apple filling into the pastry-lined pie pan mounding it in the center. Dot with butter.

On a lightly floured surface, roll out the remaining piece of pastry to a 12" round. Lightly moisten the edge of the bottom crust all around with cold water. Place the top pastry over the apples and press the two crusts together all around. Tightly roll the overhanging pastry under (all around) to make a raised edge. Flute decoratively with your fingertips or crimp with a fork. Cut three or four ¾" steam vents in the center with the tip of a paring knife.

GLAZE:
1 egg yolk
1 tsp. water
1 T. granulated sugar

In a small bowl stir together egg yolk and water. Brush the top crust (but not the fluted edge) with the egg yolk glaze twice and sprinkle with the sugar. Place pie on a baking sheet and bake for 20 minutes. Reduce oven to 350º and bake 20 to 30 minutes longer or until pie is golden brown and the apples are tender when pierced with a knife through a steam vent. Cool on a rack before serving.

Mom's Custard Pie

Pastry for 8" one-crust pie
3 eggs
1 ¾ cups milk
½ cup sugar
¼ tsp. nutmeg
1 tsp. vanilla

Heat oven to 450º. Prepare pastry. Beat eggs slightly with rotary beater. Beat in remaining ingredients. Pour into pastry-lined pie pan. Bake 20 minutes. Reduce oven temperature to 350º. Bake pie 10 minutes longer.

Bread Pudding

2 eggs, slightly beaten
2 ¼ cups milk
1 tsp. vanilla
½ tsp. cinnamon
2 cups day-old bread cut into 1" pieces
½ cup brown sugar
½ cup raisins
Salt

Combine eggs, milk, vanilla, cinnamon and salt. Stir in bread cubes, brown sugar, raisins. Pour into 8" round pan. Place in a larger shallow pan. Pour hot water into large pan. Bake at 350º for 45 minutes or until knife comes clean.

Mystery Cake of 1932

This is one of the few old recipes that can be precisely dated. It was developed in 1932 during the worst of the Depression years. In keeping with the rather desperate circumstances of that time, it contains no eggs and very little butter. The rich moist texture of the cake is most likely due to its use of tomato, a novel ingredient for a cake, but perhaps not so surprising as it may seem - the tomato, after all, is technically a fruit.

1 ½ cups all-purpose flour
1 tsp. baking soda
1 tsp. ground cinnamon
½ tsp. freshly grated nutmeg
½ tsp. ground cloves
¾ packed dark brown sugar
2 T. unsalted butter, softened
1 (10 ¾) can tomato soup
1 cup (6 oz.) raisins, chopped
½ cup (2 oz.) chopped walnuts
1 T. confectioners sugar for topping

Position a rack in the center of the oven and preheat to 350º. Grease an 11¾ x 7½ inch baking pan. In a medium sized bowl stir together flour, baking soda, cinnamon, nutmeg, and cloves. In another medium sized bowl combine the brown sugar and butter. Beat with an electric mixer until blended.

Beat in tomato soup until smooth. Stir in raisins, walnuts and dry ingredients. Turn batter into the prepared pan, smoothing the top. Bake about 30 minutes until the top springs back when lightly touched and a toothpick inserted in the center emerges clean. Cool in the pan on a rack.

If desired, arrange on top of the cake ½-inch wide strips of paper set on the diagonal in two directions to make a lattice pattern. Place confectioners sugar in a small sieve and sift over the paper. Carefully remove paper to reveal stenciled design. Cut into squares and serve. *–Jim Fobel*

Vanilla Butter Frosting

⅓ cup soft butter or margarine
3 cups confectioners' sugar
1 ½ tsp. vanilla
About 2 T. milk
2 cups coconut

Blend butter and sugar. Stir in vanilla and milk; beat until frosting is smooth and of spreading consistency. Fills and frosts two 8- or 9-inch layers.

Johnny Cake (Mom's name for cornbread)

1 ½ cups cornmeal
2 tsp. baking powder
1 tsp. salt
¼ cup shortening (Mom used bacon fat)
1 ½ cups buttermilk
½ cup all purpose flour
1 tsp. sugar
½ tsp. baking soda
2 eggs

Heat oven to 450º. Mix all ingredients. Beat vigorously for 30 seconds. Pour into two greased 8x8" pans. Bake until golden brown for 25-30 minutes.

Aunt Carolyn's Popcorn Balls

1 cup sugar
⅓ cup white corn syrup
⅓ cup water
¼ cup butter
¾ tsp. salt
2 tsp. vanilla

Aunt Carolyn

Combine all ingredients and cook slowly until temperature reaches 240º. Pop 2 cups of popcorn (more or less). Pour syrup over corn and form into balls. Air dry 2-3 hours and wrap in GLAD Press 'n Seal®.

Popcorn Balls in the bowl I sang for

Mom's Coconut Cream Pie

8" baked pie shell
¼ tsp. salt
1 T. butter, softened
½ cup sugar
2 cups milk
1 T. vanilla
3 T. cornstarch
3 eggs slightly beaten
¾ cup flaked coconut

Stir together sugar, cornstarch and salt in saucepan. Blend milk and egg yolks; gradually stir into sugar mixture. Cook over medium heat stirring constantly until mixture thickens and boils. Boil and stir 1 minute. Remove from heat; blend in butter and vanilla, stir in coconut. Immediately pour into pie shell; press plastic wrap on filling. Chill pie thoroughly, at least 2 hours. Top with meringue or whipped cream.

In 1945, Frances was a senior at Hopkins High. I was a Freshman. Guess who had all the boyfriends?

Polish Bows or *Chrusciki* (Angel Wings)

9 egg yolks
1 T. rum
½ tsp. salt
3 T. sugar
1 tsp. vanilla
Oil for deep frying
3 T. sour cream
½ tsp. baking powder
Confectioners' sugar
3½ - 4 cups flour

Beat egg yolks with sugar until well combined. Add sour cream, rum and vanilla and mix until smooth. Sift the flour, baking powder and salt. Add to egg yolk mixture a little at a time. On a heavily floured surface knead the dough vigorously punching and squeezing as much flour until the dough is no longer sticky.

Separate dough into several portions and roll very thin. Turn the dough and loosen often when rolling. Cut dough into strips approximately 1½ inches wide by 4 inches long. Tie once into loose knots or bows. Heat oil and fry quickly (only a few seconds) until golden. Turn only once. Drain on paper towels. Dust with confectioners' sugar. Makes 8 dozen.

Mom's Special Tomato Preserves

Carolyn remembers, "It was one of my Father's most favorite."

3 lbs. ripe tomatoes
2 lemons, thinly sliced
10 cups sugar
cinnamon sticks

Mix ingredients together and cook mixture until thick and clear. Place in jars. Seal. Put in water bath 15 minutes.

Genevieve

Genevieve's Pineapple Upside Down Cake

½ cup butter or margarine
1 cup firmly packed brown sugar
1 (15 ½ oz.) can pineapple slices, undrained
Maraschino cherries
2 large eggs, separated
1 cup sugar
1 cup sifted cake flour
1 tsp. baking powder
⅛ tsp. salt

Melt butter in a 10-inch cast-iron skillet. Sprinkle cherries evenly with brown sugar. Drain pineapple, reserving ⅓ cup pineapple juice; set juice aside. Arrange pineapple slices and cherries in a single layer over brown sugar.

Beat egg yolks until thick and lemon colored; gradually add sugar, beating well. Combine flour, baking powder, and salt; add to egg mixture. Stir in reserved pineapple juice.

Beat egg whites (at room temperature) until stiff peaks form; fold into flour mixture. Spoon batter evenly over pineapple slices. Bake at 375º for 30 minutes or until cake tests done. Cool for 5 minutes; invert cake onto a plate. Yield: one 10-inch cake.

THIS PAGE: **Daddy, Sister Patricia and Mom**
OPPOSITE: **Felician Motherhouse in Livonia, Michigan**

1950-1972

CONVENT DAYS

"I solemnly tell you those who have left everything and follow me will be repaid a hundredfold and will gain eternal life." —Matthew 19:27-29

The train ride to the Felician Sisters Motherhouse in Livonia, Michigan was very slow with many rosaries said. Sister Mary Patience was my escort and after the third rosary, I needed some patience. I was encouraged when some young, exuberant and happy young nuns met us at the station.

Here I was! The steps were many that led to the monumental doors of the convent. To this day I can still hear the sound of those closing doors. As I entered, a peace flowed through my body and soul and all the doubts that had beleaguered me in my high school days vanished. I knew this was my place and was truly happy.

The first year I was a Postulant and was called Sister Patricia. Our class consisted of Sisters Teresa, Stella, Julianne, Danelda, Patricia, Helen, Marlene, Stella, Iris, Maxine, Virginia, and Karen. We all attended Madonna College for a year.

There were times when I was miserably lonely. It took ten Christmases before I stopped crying for my home and family. One country song that Joe used to sing titled "The Last Letter" helped me to persevere. The words are something like this: "I cannot offer you diamonds and mansions so fine. I cannot offer you clothes that your young body craves. But if you say you long to forever be mine; think of the heartaches, the tears, and the sorrows you'll save." This was Jesus talking to me and I really did feel better.

Sweet Surrender

Raindrops line
The branches of a tree
Like strands of rosary beads.
The crystal baubles linger
Clinging to their lifelines
As I contemplate the mysteries
Of my life, bead by bead.

Hail Mary, full of grace...

Five decades to count and recite,
Five decades drenched in life,
Often achingly so,
Burying me in the dark
Of a deep
No flowers would grow.

But grow they did
Towards the light
To radiate my truths
For me,
Each one a spiraling link
To all that I am
And have yet to be.

Sorrowful, Joyful,
Glorious mysteries,
Glide through my fingers
Bead by bead,
For I have learned
Not to linger
In the pain
Life presents to me,
But to grow
In the love
And the light
That is my destiny.
–EARLENE MCMILLIN

The second year we became Novices, a totally cloistered year filled with spiritual training, no home visits, no letters, just Jesus. We were given new names to tell the world we were a new person! We were given three choices and my first choice was "Nadine." Sister Mary Emmanuel, a Council Member who coaxed my vocation, approved my first choice.

Sister Nadine and Sister de Lourdes (Julie W.), 1958. Nun better.

"Come, Bride of Christ, and receive the crown which the Lord has prepared for you forever. –REV 2:8

The third year we received the black veil and were now full-fledged nuns. I continued my college education and was sent to teach 50 second graders at St. Michael School, Livonia, Michigan. I was 20 years old and totally unprepared. However, Jesus was always near in two special Felicians, Sisters Mary Inez and Mary Immaculata, who gave me all the help I desperately needed. I continued my education, graduated from Madonna College, and began a Master's program at Wayne State in Detroit. I chose to study Foods and Nutrition, Clothing and Textiles as I did in college.

Graduating from Wayne State allowed me to teach in the upper grades and in high school. I found great joy in being Sister Nadine. I loved the convent, the prayers, the big city churches, the singing and the friends I made among students and other nuns. Teaching was always challenging and satisfying. Feeling a sense of accomplishment was good. So I continued teaching subjects in my field.

"Try to recognize and realize the splendor of being clothed from within, of being adorned with the life, light and love of My Spirit."

23

THIS PAGE: **Sister Nadine and Sister Angeline**
OPPOSITE: **Jim and Angel Erdmans**

The Angel Story:
Joy and Sorrow and Joy

In 1956 a totally unexpected event occurred — pure joy and delight! My sister Angel entered the convent. It was here that we became better than best friends. I was so happy that I wrote this poem when she entered.

Just An Exchange
The home I love with Mom and Dad
no longer will I see.
For another home now takes its place,
a home built with love for me!
I leave the worldly pleasures
with all their passing fancy,
to receive happiness from living
just with Thee!

My sisters each one I love so dearly.
Will now be replaced by 800 nearly!
And although I realize that
nothing I'll truly possess
Still with the thought of Christ
My heart is singing with untold
happiness.
—NADINE BEGIN

From the moment she walked in the convent there were hugs and tears, laughter, music and joy ever after. Any time we could spend together we did. Reverend Mother assigned us to Guardian Angel Orphanage. We had the time of our life dodging the ghosts of the nuns who died there.

Her time in the convent was spent going to college. We managed any good time we could. Her first year was almost over. Another twist and turn! She became ill and no longer could remain here. There were tears, hugs and deep sadness. She wanted desperately to be a nun. Today we are still the best of friends. She married a wonderful husband and is the mother of six children and 11 grandchildren.

"During my year in the convent I learned two very important lessons. The first lesson was that our Lord is always there to help, allowing me to trust Him and have my faith grow continually. Secondly, during that year in the convent Nadine and I became very close. Now we have a mutual love for Jesus, music, laughter, crying, and just life. This connection is truly amazing to me and for this I am eternally grateful."—ANGEL

Praise the Lord
"Life is better left to chance. We could have missed the pain but would have missed the dance."

We danced. We were happy. The dance continued....

Spending a summer in Berea, Kentucky working with Father Beiting's organization was

25

Rev. Robert Begin

indeed a joy. Volunteers from all over the United States met and received various jobs working with the poor of Appalachia. My job was to work in the Thrift Center. It was the first time in 20 years that I wore lay clothes so, of course I was asked, "How come you all aren't marred (married)?" My reply, "I am, and His name is Jesus."

Upon my return Reverend Mother assigned me to St. Mary's Hospital as a food supervisor. Great joy! I needed a new job. I had been teaching for 20 years in various schools in Bay City, in Detroit, and in Livonia. With delight in my heart, I reported for duty only to discover that the hospital administrator had already replaced me with another Sister. Suitcase in hand I walked back to the Motherhouse. Some friends offered me a ride with these words, "Only you, Nadine, could be fired at 7:30 in the morning."

✻   ✻   ✻

The moon decorating the sea with a highway of lights, the powerful sound of the waves pushing against the ship tells me that we have left Mt. Etna in Sicily and are now destined for Monte Carlo. The Venetian Lace is transformed into a mountainous heap of meringue. As I watch the transforming and rearranging waves of the beckoning ocean, I began to think – is this ocean my Fortune Teller?

✻   ✻   ✻

"He asks us to let go of the reasons and throw our arms around His neck."–BRUCE WILKINSON

There are times in our lives when fate takes over. Little did I know that the administrator's rejection would lead to a new life beyond any expectations or dreams. Back to Reverend Mother I return!

In the 1970s many religious orders were undergoing change. More freedom was allowed, absence of the habit and restrictive guidance of a Superior. The Felicians allowed an experimental group and were in search of one more person to join them. We maintained our vows of poverty, chastity, and obedience and were allowed lay dress and choice of an apostolate.

The convent and church was St. Margaret Mary, Detroit, Michigan, and an available job at Nativity High School provided me with another year of teaching Home Economics. Just like the uncontrollable waves of the ocean twisting and turning, my life was about to change.

> *"Let choice whisper in your ear and love murmur in your heart.*
> *Be ready. Here comes Life!"*
> —MAYA ANGELOU

Introducing ourselves to the pastor, Reverend Robert Begin, we found a handsome, debonair French priest descending the church steps. We were warmly greeted. In the 1970s community life was popular. Our group consisted of religious Brothers, married couples, and employees of Brothers Construction with Rev. Begin in charge.

Every morning we attended Mass and at the end of the day we enjoyed a community meal. St. Margaret Mary's was great with many wonderful people. This experiment of a more independent lifestyle was a success. We found we could still be devoted to Christ with fewer shackles.

Those ever-churning and moving waves were presenting us with another challenge. The hospital administrator was appointed Reverend Mother and called us back to the convent. There was finality in her voice. "You either come back, wear the habit, do what we want you to do, go where we tell you to go, or LEAVE." It was a shock since many other religious orders allowed these changes.

Finding it impossible to fulfill these requests, we left and continued to work at St. Margaret Mary another year waiting for Rome to send our dispensation from our vows. I was happy

Sister Nadine

working at the parish teaching sewing to the neighborhood ladies, preparing dinner for our community, taking parish census and visiting the sick. With the completion of the second year, I moved to an apartment in Royal Oak, Michigan.

My brother has always been the most faithful friend you can imagine. Throughout my convent years Joe had been there for me writing beautiful letters of encouragement, visiting, and sharing his loving family. After I left and moved to an apartment, he was there to help me buy a red Duster car with the words, "Yesterday is dead and gone." I taught school one more year at Bishop Foley in Madison Heights, Michigan.

"I am not afraid of tomorrow
For I have seen yesterday
And I love today."

This span of 22 years was filled with education, spiritual and secular, teaching, praying, singing and many unexpected and radical changes.

Awakening
Raindrops cling
To my window
Like stars
Fixed in the heavens,
Silver drops
Of separate selves
Holding to their
Thoughts and schemes.
An explosion of thunder
Shatters their dreams
And they trickle down
In ribbons of streams
To merge within
Another's dreams
Splashing rings
Of possibilities
As endless as the stars.
–EARLENE MCMILLIN

The Recipes

In 1950-1953 we had beautiful ceremonies becoming Novices, receiving the white veil and then the black veil as fully professed Sisters. Our family and friends were invited. It was the joy of a wedding. Everyone's most favorite food was "babka" which Sister Isadore would bake in her mountainous ovens. It was served with humble bologna.

When we were sent to the missions we sometimes had to take turns cooking if no one was designated. Teaching foods and nutrition in high schools and summer jobs at Orchard Lake and Saint Francis Nursing Home in Saginaw, Michigan, provided me with many challenging experiences.

1950-1972
RECIPES

SOUPS & SALADS
Beet Soup *(Barszcz)*
Sauerkraut Soup *(Kapusta)*
Uptown Convent Fruit Soup

MEATS & VEGETABLES
Meatloaf
Stuffed Cabbage Rolls *(Golabki)*
Turkey Paprika with *Kluski*
Easy Noodles *(Kluski)*

BREAD, PASTRY, DESSERTS
Convent *Babka*
Small *Babka*
Kolacky
Polish Donuts *(Paczki)*
Poppy Seed Roll

Convent Babka (RECIPE PG 34)

Beet Soup *(Barszcz)*

1 large meaty beef soup bone
1 ½ lbs beets, peeled and sliced ⅛" thick
1 large chopped onion
4 tsp. salt
1 ½ tsp. whole allspice
½ cup cider vinegar
1 cup sour cream
¼ cup flour
Hot cooked noodles (See recipe on pg. 33
   for easy noodles or use commercial)

In a large kettle gently boil soup bone in water, uncovered for 1 hour or until meat is tender. Skim carefully. Add beets, onions, salt and all-spice; bring to a boil. Cook uncovered over medium heat until beets are tender, about 25-30 minutes. Remove bone, cut meat in bite-size pieces and return to soup. (Discard bone.) Add ½ cup vinegar. Blend sour cream and flour until smooth; add soup broth to form a thin paste, then gradually stir into soup. Cook and stir until mixture begins to boil. Serve with noodles. Makes about 3 quarts.

NOTE: Soup should be pleasantly sweet-sour. If desired, add more vinegar to taste.

Sauerkraut Soup *(Kapusta)*

2 lbs lean pork neck bones
2 cans (27 oz. each) sauerkraut rinsed, if
   desired
1 c pearl barley
1 large chopped onion
1 tsp. caraway seed

In a large kettle boil bones in 2 quarts water, uncovered for 1 hour. Skim carefully. Add 2 cups water and remaining ingredients; cover and cook over low heat 1 hour or until meat on bones and barley are tender. Discard bones. Add more water or wine if needed. Makes about three quarts.

NOTE: *Kapusta* is similar to chowder. It will thicken with storage in refrigerator. Thin with a little hot broth if desired.

Uptown Convent Fruit Soup

2 cups water
2 cups sweet white wine, such as a
   Gewurztraminer
½ cup sugar
Zest of one orange, removed in strips with
   a vegetable peeler
Zest of one lime, removed in strips with a
   vegetable peeler
Pinch of Chinese 5-spice powder
Small bunch of fresh mint leaves
½ cup fresh diced pineapple
3 fresh kiwis, peeled, diced
½ cup fresh papaya, peeled, diced
½ cup fresh mango, peeled, diced
½ cup fresh blackberries or blueberries
½ cup fresh raspberries
3 cloves

Combine water, wine, sugar, orange and lime peels, 5-spice powder, cloves and mint in a non-reactive saucepan over low heat; bring to a simmer and then remove from the heat. Allow to steep for at least 1 hour. Strain through a fine mesh sieve and place in a covered container. *To serve:* Ladle into bowls and garnish with all of the fresh fruit listed. May be stored in the refrigerator for up to 1 week. Serves 4

Meatloaf

2 eggs
½ cup chopped onion
¼ tsp. pepper
⅔ cup milk
½ cup grated carrot
1 ½ lbs. lean ground beef
3 slices bread, torn into pieces
1 tsp. salt
1 T. chopped fresh parsley or 1 tsp. dried
   parsley
1 cup (4 oz.) shredded cheddar or mozzarella cheese
1 tsp. dried basil, thyme or sage, optional

TOPPING:
½ **cup tomato sauce**
½ **cup packed brown sugar**
1 **tsp. prepared mustard**

In a large bowl, beat eggs. Add milk and bread; let stand a few minutes or until the bread absorbs the liquid. Stir in onion, carrot, cheese, herbs and seasonings. Add beef and mix well. In a shallow baking pan, shape beef mixture into a 7 ½ x 3 ½ x 2 ½ - inch loaf. Bake at 350° for 45 minutes.

Meanwhile combine topping ingredients. Spoon some of the topping over meat loaf. Bake for about 30 minutes longer or until no pink remains, occasionally spooning some of the remaining topping over loaf. Let stand 10 minutes before serving.

Stuffed Cabbage Rolls (*Golabki*)

1 **head cabbage**
1 **lb. ground beef**
½ **lb. ground pork (or veal)**
16 **oz. can tomato sauce**
8 **oz. can tomatoes**
Salt & pepper to taste
2 **cups cooked rice**
2 **eggs**
1 **onion finely chopped**
2 **T. margarine**
2 **T. brown sugar**
½ **lb. lean bacon**

Remove core from cabbage. Scald cabbage in boiling water and remove leaves as they soften. Sauté onions in margarine very lightly; do not brown. Combine meat with rice, eggs, and seasoning. Mix well.

Place 2 T. of mixture in center of cabbage leaf and roll. Wrap in bacon strips and insert wooden picks to hold together. Pour tomato sauce on rolls, then squeeze tomatoes from can and arrange on top of rolls. Sprinkle brown sugar and bake at 350° for 1 hour or until done.

Turkey Paprika with Easy Noodles (*Kluski*)

1 **cup fresh mushrooms, sliced**
2 **T. butter**
2 **T. flour**
1 **cup sour cream**
1 **can (10 oz.) cream of mushroom soup**
1 **can (15 oz.) artichoke hearts, drained and halved**
3 **T. Parmesan cheese, grated**
2 ½ **cups cooked chicken, ham or turkey**
¼ **cup slivered almonds, toasted**
⅓ **cup white wine**
¼ **T. paprika and** ¼ **cup pimento**

In a saucepan, cook mushrooms in butter and push to one side. Add flour to make a roux. Cook a minute, then add sour cream. Cook over low heat until thickened, stirring constantly. Blend in soup, wine and cheese. Add chicken and artichokes; heat through. Stir gently. Serve from a chafing dish. Garnish with almonds and pimentos, and pour over pastry shells or toast . Can also be combined with *Kluski* (Easy Noodles).

Easy Noodles (*Kluski*)

3 **egg yolks**
½ **cup cold water**
About 1 cup flour to form soft dough
Boiling water
Salt

Beat egg yolks, ½ tsp. salt and cold water. Stir in flour and knead until dough is smooth and elastic. Roll up as for jelly roll and cut into strips. Cook in salted boiling water for 5 minutes. Drain and serve.

Convent *Babka*

This recipe makes two 9-inch springform cakes.

2 cups milk, scalded, 85º
½ lb. (2 sticks) unsalted butter
4 tsp. dry yeast
¼ cup warm water (100-115º)
4 eggs
4 egg yolks
1 cup sugar
2 tsp. salt
Grated rind of 2 oranges
Grated rind of 1 lemon
1 tsp. vanilla
1 T. vodka
8 to 9 cups sifted unbleached flour
2 cups golden raisins

TOPPING CRUMBS:
Mix ⅓ cup sugar
2 to 5 T. flour
3 T. butter
1 tsp. vanilla
Few tsp. orange peel

Heat the milk; stir in the butter until melted; cool to lukewarm. Proof the yeast in the warm water.

Beat the eggs, egg yolks, and sugar until thick. Add the salt, grated rinds, vanilla, and Vodka. Add the milk-butter mixture to the egg mixture. Stir in the yeast.

Add the flour, a cupful at a time, mixing with a wooden spoon. The dough should not be dry, but it should not be sticky. Too much flour will make a dry, crumbly cake. Add the raisins.

Turn the dough onto a floured board and knead for about 5 minutes, until dough comes away from your hand. Butter a very large bowl and put dough in bowl. Cover and let rise in a 130º oven until doubled in bulk. Punch down and let rise a second time until almost doubled.

Preheat oven to 350º. Butter the pans generously. Divide the dough into 2 portions. Arrange evenly in the pans and cover loosely. Add topping. Let rise until doubled. Add topping crumbs.

Bake cakes in oven for 30 to 45 minutes, until golden brown. There should be a hollow sound when you rap the top with your knuckles. Cool for 5 minutes in the pans, then turn out onto racks to cool. Serve warm.

Small *Babka*

¾ cup hot milk
2 cups flour
1 yeast cake
1 T. warm water
2 T. soft butter
⅓ cup sugar
½ tsp. salt
2 egg yolks
½ tsp. cardamon, optional
Ground raisins, optional
Chopped nuts, optional
Chopped cherries, optional

Scald milk. Carefully stir ½ cup of flour into hot milk. When smooth and cool, add yeast softened in warm water with 1 tsp. sugar. Set aside to rise.

Add salt to egg yolks and beat until thick. Add to "sponge" the butter, sugar, beaten egg yolks and cardamon. Beat with spoon thoroughly. Slowly add the remaining 1 ½ cups of flour and knead with hand until dough no longer sticks to the fingers; add raisins, nuts and cherries, if wished. Let rise until double in bulk. Punch down and let rise again, about 1 hour.

Bake in greased loaf, tube, or sheet pan to suit your fancy. Let dough rise until about double in size after placing in pan. Bake for 30 minutes at 350º. —*Sister Mary Euphrasia, Enfield, CT*

Kolacky

1 cup butter or margarine, softened
1 pkg (8 oz.) cream cheese, softened
¼ tsp. vanilla extract
2 ¼ cups flour
½ tsp. salt
Thick jam or canned fruit filling (apricot
   or prune)

Cream butter and cream cheese until fluffy. Beat in vanilla extract. Combine flour and salt. Add in fourths to butter mixture blending well after each addition. Chill dough until easy to handle. Roll dough to ⅜ inch thick on a floured surface. Cut out 2-inch circles or other shapes. Place on an ungreased cookie sheet. Make a "thumb print" about ¼ inch deep in each. Fill with jam. Bake at 350º for 10 to 15 minutes or until delicately browned on edges. Makes about 3 ½ dozen.

Polish Donuts (Paczki)

1 pkg. active dry yeast
¼ cup warm water
⅓ cup butter, softened
1 egg
3 ½ cups flour
Confectioners sugar, optional
1 tsp. vanilla extract
1 tsp. grated orange or lemon peel
⅔ cup sugar
3 egg yolks
Fat for deep frying heated to 375º

Stir yeast in warm water. Cream butter and sugar until fluffy. Beat in egg, then egg yolks, one at a time. Add vanilla extract, orange peel, dissolved yeast and salt. Beat until well mixed.

Stir in flour gradually, adding enough to make a stiff dough. Turn dough onto a floured surface. Knead until smooth and elastic, about 10 min. Place in a greased bowl. Cover. Let rise until doubled in bulk. Turn onto lightly floured surface. Pat or roll to ½ inch thick. Cut out with a donut cutter. Cover. Let rise until doubled in bulk.

Fry in hot fat 2 to 3 minutes; turn to brown all sides. Drain donuts on paper towels and sprinkle with confectioners sugar, if desired. Makes about 2 dozen.

Poppy Seed Roll

5-6 cups all-purpose flour
2 pkgs. active dry yeast
1½ cups milk
⅓ cup sugar
⅓ cup shortening
2 eggs
Poppy seed filling

In a large mixer bowl combine 2 cups of the flour and yeast. Heat milk, sugar, shortening and 1 tsp. salt until warm (115-120º) stirring constantly to melt shortening. Add to dry mixture, add eggs. Beat at low speed with electric mixer for ½ minute, scraping bowl. Beat 3 minutes at high speed. By hand stir in enough remaining flour to make a moderately stiff dough.

Turn out on floured surface and knead until smooth and elastic 5-10 minutes. Shape into ball and place in greased bowl; turn one. Cover, let rise in warm place until double (1 to 1 ¾ hours). Punch down dough and divide in half. Cover; let rest 10 minutes.

On floured surface, roll each half to 24x8-inch rectangle. Spread each with half the poppy seed filling. Roll up, starting at short end and seal long ends. Place seam-side down in greased 9x5x3-inch loaf pans. Cover, let rise until double (30 to 45 minutes). Bake at 350º for 35 to 40 minutes. Remove from pans and cool. Makes 2 loaves.

POPPY SEED FILLING:
Pour 1 cup boiling water over ¾ cup poppy seed (4 oz.) and drain. Cover with 1 cup lukewarm water and let stand 30 minutes. Drain thoroughly. Grind poppy seed in blender or use the finest blade of a food grinder. Stir in ½ cup chopped nuts, ½ cup honey, and 1 tsp. grated lemon peel. Fold 1 stiffly beaten egg white into filling mixture.

NOTE: Ready-made Solo Poppy Seed Cake and Pastry Filling can be purchased.

THIS PAGE: **Me in Hawaii, 1980**
OPPOSITE: **Wedding Day**

1972-1980

JUST NADINE, DETROIT AND MARRIAGE

So here I was - totally free - 40 years old and for the first time on my own. Temporary elation - my life was one of giving and I knew this was a momentary freedom. For fun, a few friends of mine in the same situation would go dancing at the singles club. I found myself on a date with a guy who was 21. Many told me that I looked ten years younger, but this was stretching it a bit. There was Robert - still a priest but had requested laicization from Rome. I had no high hopes; a broken heart was not a twist I wanted to deal with. So I continued to work teaching at Bishop Foley.

One night I received a telephone call. My heart sank and almost stopped. I recognized Bob's voice, " Would you like a little company tonight?" Dead silence for half a moment. What was I waiting for? "Yes. Yes!" This was the beginning of another beautiful love. Jesus has always been there but this was a whole new horizon. As circumstances changed in my life over which I had no control, I pondered the thought. I can love both! A twist and turn and I knew which way to go.

"You rose into my life like a promised sunrise,
brightening my days with the light
in your eyes.
I've never been so strong.
Now I'm where I belong."
—MAYA ANGELOU

Robert was waiting for the formal documents of laicization —once a priest; always a priest, but sadly to say unable to function publicly as a priest. Friday night became a special time for us usually a dinner at a fine restaurant.

It was somewhere in the third year we drove to the *Ye Ole Steakhouse* in Windsor, Canada. On the way Bob showed me a picture of a beautiful house on Hamilton Drive, the backyard was the Detroit Golf Club. That night as we sat in front of the fireplace holding a glass of wine, he proposed: *"Je vous aime cherie avec tout mon coeur. Je veux demeurer avec vous pour toute ma view. Voulez-vous faire le meme?"* [I love you, dear, with all my heart. I want to live with you all my life. Would you like to do the same?]

"Say it in English." I wanted to jump on the table and dance my heart out. Disbelief turned into pure joy. Many popular songs in the 1970s expressed my deep elation: *"I'm the Happiest Girl in the whole USA"* and *"I'm on the Top of the World"*.

The Birth of Love
Swirling through
Celestial space
Our love was born
On the breath of dawn.
Perfect in form,
Divine in inspiration,
Weathering any earthly storm.

We celebrated our love and marriage on October 4, 1974, the Feast of St. Francis and Robert's 41st birthday. I wore a beautiful turquoise gown; Bob a tuxedo. My brother Joe escorted me into the spacious family room of the Hamilton House with these words to Bob,

Hamilton House, Detroit, Michigan

THIS PAGE: **Honeymoon, Mexico, 1974.**
*It takes that good woman to make
a good man better.*—DAN MATEY

"You take over." Everyone sang *"Today While the Blossoms still Cling to the Vine."* My sister Angel was my Maid of Honor and two priests married us: Joe Hopkins and Bill Downey.

The choir from Gesu Church sang and my dearest Mother, who was thrilled when I became a nun, was now thoroughly excited about my wonderful future life. We had a huge tent in the backyard and the band started playing 100 of my favorite songs ... *"Quantanamera," "Somewhere My Love"* and on and on.

That night we left our house as Mr. and Mrs. Begin and honeymooned in Acapulco. Upon our return Robert assumed his position as CEO for Matvest, a company that he started as a non-profit organization called Brother's Construction. Time for another twist and turn.

We deeply wanted to have a child; no luck. My youngest sister Mari was going through a sad divorce. She needed time to complete her education. It did not look like a pregnancy was possible. Not wanting to be selfish we invited three of her children to live with us for a period of two years. The twist and turn was more than we anticipated. Here I was – instant Motherhood. It was a beautiful two years.

After six months, Jeanmarie, 15, decided to return to her mother. Beth was in the seventh grade and Charlie in the third. The two years they stayed were years filled with much joy and love: the Halloween parties, Christmases, Beth's Confirmation and Charlie's First Communion. I made Charlie a light blue suit so that he could welcome the Lord in fine array. Lo and Behold! It was during this time that I became pregnant. "Dear Jesus, did I have to do this for You to bless us with a child?" I guess ...

Marie Chantal
Past the moon
And beyond the stars
The angels did sing
The heavens leaned in,
So full was the joy
On the birth of our child.
I smile and weep in turn
Be humbled am I,
Our precious daughter to receive
To hold against my breast,
For deep was my longing
And fervent my prayers
To be blessed with the gift
Of motherhood.
Asleep, she lies in grateful arms
Resting near my heart.
Keeping watch I'll tenderly be
Like the good Shepherd
Who looks after His lambs.
–EARLENE MCMILLIN

Robert announced to everyone "Nadine, like Sarah of old, is with child." It was during Beth and Charlie's stay that Marie Chantal was born on March 10, 1978. Talk about elation! I was blessed with many beautiful happenings: becoming a nun, receiving the veil, my wedding day... However, nothing on earth can compare to the ecstasy of God's presence as when this beautiful baby with darting brown eyes was placed in my arms. Beth, my niece, ran down

Marie-Chantal, Me and Robert, 1978

Beth, Charlie, Marie-Chantal

Marie-Chantal's First Thanksgiving, with Grandmother Rose Begin

Hamilton Drive publicly announcing to all the neighbors, "My Aunt had a baby girl! My Aunt had a baby girl!"

So there we were—our very own child and Beth and Charlie's two year period was up. The two were going back to live with their mother. Talk about sad. All of us cried. Charlie never failed to say, "Aunt Nadine, you are so beautiful." These were two good years for all of us.

Life was good. I had a wonderful husband, a beautiful child, I lived on a street easily accessible to Somerset, Birmingham, Fisher Theater, fine restaurants, and many friends. Having Thanksgiving dinners, company, Birthday and Halloween parties, weddings and baptisms kept me current in my profession.

Time for another twist and turn. Yes, indeed. Robert had been working in the city for many years and was ready for a new challenge, a new dream, a new accomplishment. What a dream! Listen... "Move to Traverse City, buy a farm, plant a vineyard, build a winery and a twelve room inn. Woe is me." The words I said "I DO" are coming back to haunt me.

We sold our beautiful Hamilton House and said farewell to friends, Somerset, Fisher Theater, etc., etc., etc.

Surfs up
In your sky of blue.
Don your cloud walking gear
For leaps of faith
And roads less traveled by.
No cloud clogging statisticians
To chart your course,
No maps,
No boundaries,
No rhumb lines,
As the sailors say,
Only billowing puffs
To float upon
And pearl white crests
To mount and climb.
—EARLENE MCMILLIN

Mari

The Recipes

A short period but one filled with a tremendous jubilant change. All my education and experiences were certainly put to a test.

The first challenge was Thanksgiving dinner for both of our families. The walls of the Hamilton House were bursting with laughter, joy and love. In addition, our friends used our home for wedding receptions and baptisms.

There were many parties - the Company, Matvest, Halloween and birthdays. The best part, of course, the children — Charlie, Beth, and Baby Chantal.

The following is a sampling of foods prepared and served.

1972-1980

RECIPES

APERITIF
Mock Champagne Punch
Shrimp Cocktail with Brandy and Cream

SOUPS
French Canadian Pea Soup
Oyster Stew

MAIN DISHES
Baked Stuffed Pike
Lasagne
Bodega Shrimp au Gratin
Roasted Capons with Oyster & Rice Stuffing
Brandy-Buttered Roast Turkey
Herb-Crusted Prime Rib with Port
  Wine Sauce
Liver & Veal Loaf

VEGETABLES & SIDE DISHES
Sausage Bread Stuffing
Oyster Dressing
Cranberry Sauce with Port & Tangerine
Double Baked Roquefort Potatoes
Old-Fashioned Corn Relish
Sweet Potato Fries

BREAD, PASTRY, DESSERTS
Creamy Rice Pudding
Angel Erdman's Ribbon Gelatin
Bananas Foster Shortcake
Elaine's Pie Crust
Grand Marnier Baked Custard
VIP Pecan Pie
Sanders Refrigerator Rolls
Sanders Coffee Cake & Streusel Topping
Sanders Butter Frosting
Sanders Glossy Chocolate Fudge Icing
Sanders Hot Fudge Topping

Mock Champagne Punch (RECIPE ON PG. 46)

Mock Champagne Punch

3 (6 oz.) cans frozen orange juice
concentrate, thawed
3 (6 oz.) cans frozen grapefruit juice
concentrate, thawed
2 (18 oz.) cans pineapple juice, chilled
2 cups cranberry juice
3 (28 fluid oz.) ginger ale, chilled

Place orange and grapefruit concentrate, pineapple juice, and cranberry juice in a punch bowl. Just before serving, add ginger ale and mix. If desired, float a few fresh strawberries. Makes 32 ½ cups or 4 quarts.
—Irma Macy

Shrimp Cocktail with Brandy and Cream

36 cooked fresh shrimp
1 hard boiled egg yolk
1 tsp. Dijon mustard
3 T. olive oil
1 tsp. lemon juice
6 T. chili sauce
2-3 drops Worcestershire sauce
1 T. brandy
2 T. cream
½ tsp. salt
Freshly ground pepper to taste

Mash egg yolk and mustard in a bowl. Add 2 T. of oil drop-by-drop stirring constantly as if you were making mayonnaise. Gradually add lemon juice and remaining oil. Stir in remaining ingredients. Chill and serve with shrimp.

French Canadian Pea Soup

1 lb. (2 cups) dried yellow split peas
12 cups water
1 ham bone
1 cup chopped onions
½ cup chopped celery
1 ½ tsp. salt
2 chopped shallots (green onions)
½ tsp. pepper
½ tsp. dried savory leaves
1 or 2 potatoes (chopped or small cubes)
1 bay leaf

Wash peas and soak overnight in 4 cups of cold water. Drain. Add the 12 cups of water, ham bone, celery, potatoes and seasonings. Cover, bring to a boil and simmer until peas are tender (about 2 hours). Remove ham bone and take off meat. Return meat to soup. (Add more water if needed during cooking.) —Jacquie Begin

Oyster Stew

2 T. each minced celery and onion
4 T. butter or margarine
2 T. flour
½ tsp. salt
⅛ tsp. pepper
3 cups milk
1 pint oysters with their liquor
1 cup heavy cream
Mace to taste
Chopped green onion to taste (optional)

In a 3-quart saucepan sauté celery and onion in butter 5 minutes until tender, stirring occasionally. Remove from heat. Stir in flour, salt and pepper. Gradually stir in milk, then cook and stir until thickened. Add oysters with liquor and cream. Stir over low heat 5 minutes or just until edges of oysters begin to curl. Sprinkle with mace and onion. Makes 6-8 servings.

Baked Stuffed Pike

3 T. butter plus 2 T. butter softened
½ cup finely chopped onions
1 ½ cups fresh soft crumbs, made from
    homemade-type white bread, pulverized
    with a blender or shredded with a fork
2 T. finely chopped parsley
2 T. milk
½ tsp. finely grated lemon peel
1 cup red Bordeaux or other dry red wine
    combined with ½ cup fresh orange juice
1 tsp. crumbled dried sage leaves
Salt
Freshly ground black pepper
1 large garlic clove, peeled and bruised
    with the
    flat side of a heavy knife
3 lb. whole pike, cleaned and scaled but
    with head and tail left on, or substitute
    any other whole 3 lb. firm white fish

In a heavy 6 to 8-inch skillet, melt the 3 T. of butter over moderate heat, add the onions and cook, stirring constantly for 5 minutes or until they are soft and transparent but not brown.

With a rubber spatula transfer them to a large mixing bowl and stir in the bread crumbs, parsley, 2 T. of milk, lemon peel, sage, ¼ tsp of salt and a few grindings of pepper. Taste for seasoning and set aside.

Preheat oven to 350º. Rub the bruised garlic over the bottom and sides of a shallow baking and serving dish just large enough to hold the fish comfortably. With a pastry brush, coat the bottom of the dish with 1 T. of the softened butter.

Wash the fish inside and out under cold running water and dry it thoroughly with paper towels. Loosely fill the cavity of the fish with the stuffing, then close the opening with small skewers crisscrossing them with kitchen cord as if lacing a turkey.

Brush the fish with remaining T. of softened butter and sprinkle it with salt and a few grindings of pepper. Place fish in baking dish and pour in the combined wine and orange juice.

Bake uncovered in the middle of the oven for 30 to 40 minutes basting every 10 minutes with the pan liquid. The fish is done when its flesh is firm to the touch. Serve at once directly from the baking dish moistening each serving with a little of the sauce. Serves 4 to 6.

Lasagne

1 lb. ground beef or Italian sausage
1 clove garlic, minced
1 T. whole basil
1 ½ tsp. salt
1 lb. can (2 cups) whole tomatoes
1 (6 oz.) can tomato paste
10 oz. lasagne wide noodles
3 cups Ricotta or creamy cottage cheese
2 T. parsley flakes
2 beaten eggs
2 tsp. salt and ½ tsp. pepper
1 lb. mozzarella cheese, sliced very thin

Brown meat slowly; spoon off excess fat. Add next 5 ingredients. Simmer uncovered 30 minutes, stirring occasionally. Cook noodles in large amount of boiling salted water until tender; drain; rinse. (Hint: to keep noodles from sticking together add 1 or 2 T. of oil in water). Combine remaining ingredients except mozzarella cheese.

Place half the noodles in 13x9x2 inch baking dish; spread with half the cottage cheese filling; add half the mozzarella cheese and half the meat sauce. Repeat layers. Bake at 375º about 30 minutes. Let stand 10 minutes before cutting into squares. Filling will set slightly. Serves 12. –Jacquie Begin

Bodega Shrimp Au Gratin

Bodega Shrimp au Gratin

from the Bodega Restaurant

1 pkg (6 oz.) long-grain wild rice, prepared
  according to package directions
2 cans (4 oz. each) mushroom stems and
  pieces, drained
½ cup green peas, cooked
½ cup grated Parmesan cheese
1 tsp. white pepper
½ tsp. garlic powder
2 T. butter
2 T. flour
2 cups half & half
2 T. sherry
1 tsp. light corn syrup
½ tsp. lemon juice
Dash liquid hot pepper sauce
2 oz. American cheese spread
2 oz. cold-pack Cheddar cheese
3 T. grated Parmesan cheese
1 ¼ lbs. cooked shrimp, shelled
  and deveined
½ cup seasoned stuffing crumbs

Prepare rice mixture; mix together cooked rice, mushrooms, peas, ½ cup Parmesan cheese, white pepper and garlic powder. Set aside.

Prepare cheese sauce: In saucepan, melt butter. Stir in flour and cook until bubbly. Gradually add half & half, sherry, corn syrup, lemon juice and liquid hot pepper sauce. Cook, stirring constantly until thick. Remove from heat. Stir in processed cheese spread, Cheddar cheese and 2 T. Parmesan cheese until melted. Set aside.

Cover bottom of 13x9x12-inch baking dish with rice mixture. Top with shrimp. Pour cheese over all. Sprinkle with stuffing crumbs. Bake in 375º oven for 20 minutes or until sauce is slightly browned. Makes 6-8 servings.

Roasted Capons with Oyster and Rice Stuffing

OYSTER AND RICE STUFFING:
2 cups finely chopped onion
1 cup finely chopped celery
1 ½ cups (3 sticks) butter (less may be
  used)
6 cups cooked white rice
½ cup finely chopped parsley
1 tsp. salt
½ tsp. pepper
1 ½ pints shucked oyster in their liquor
1 egg, slightly beaten
2 capons (about 6 lbs. each)
Half lemon
¼ cup currant jelly
2 T. water

Saute onion and celery in 1 cup of the butter in a large saucepan until onion is softened, 3 minutes. Remove from heat. Stir in rice, parsley, salt and pepper. Drain liquor from oysters into small saucepan; reserve oysters. Bring liquor just to boiling. Halve oysters if large; add to liquid. Cook about 1 minute or until edges of oysters just begin to curl. Drain. Stir oysters into rice mixture. Cool mixture slightly. Stir in egg.

CAPONS:

Melt remaining ½ cup butter in small saucepan, reserve. Preheat oven to 375º. Rinse capons. Pat dry inside and out with paper toweling. Rub interior with lemon. Boil necks, gizzards, hearts, and livers to make stock for gravy. Stuff neck and body cavities with stuffing. Close cavities with string and skewers or by sewing with heavy white thread. Prick legs and backs of capons. Place on rack in shallow roasting pan.

Roast in preheated moderate oven (375º) for 2 hours or until leg joint moves easily and juices run clear; baste with pan juices and melted butter every 30 minutes. Heat currant jelly and water in small saucepan until jelly melts. Brush capons with glaze and return to oven for 5 minutes longer. Makes 16 servings.

Brandy-Buttered Roast Turkey

1 ready-to-cook turkey, 12 to 14 lbs.
Salt and pepper
½ cup Christian Brothers Brandy
Oil
½ cup butter

Rub body and neck cavities of turkey lightly with salt and pepper. If desired, fill cavities loosely with preferred stuffing (or stuffing can be baked in a covered casserole last hour turkey roasts, if preferred). Skewer opening, tie legs close to body and turn wing tips back under body. Place on rack in shallow roasting pan.

Brush skin with oil. Roast in moderately slow oven (325º) about 1 ½ hours until skin begins to color. Melt butter and add brandy. Baste turkey with brandy-butter about every 20 minutes continuing to roast about 2 to 2 ½ hours longer, until drumstick can be moved up and down easily and fleshy part of drumstick feels very soft and tender when pressed with fingers protected with a folded paper towel. Makes 8 to 10 servings.

Herb-Crusted Prime Rib with Port Wine Sauce

1 T. coarsely ground black pepper
1 T. chopped fresh parsley
2 tsp. chopped fresh rosemary
1 tsp. chopped fresh thyme
1 tsp. minced garlic
1 tsp. salt
2 tsp. water
7-8 lbs. oven-ready prime rib (3 ribs)
2 cups ruby port
4 cups veal or beef broth
2 tsp. cornstarch
Portabella mushrooms

Preheat oven to 350º. In a bowl, combine pepper, parsley, rosemary, thyme, garlic and salt, and mix well. Set roast on a cutting board and rub mixture evenly over entire surface of meat. Place meat on a rack in a roasting pan, and cook until an instant-read thermometer inserted into the center of the meat registers 120-125º for very rare to medium-rare (2-2 ¼ hours); 130-135º for medium to medium well (2 ¼-2 ¾ hours).

Let meat stand 12-20 minutes before carving. Meanwhile, in a saucepan over medium-low heat, combine port and veal broth. Cook and stir until liquid is reduced to 1 cup (10-12 minutes). Skim fat from roasting pan. In a bowl, whisk together cornstarch and water, add to reduced liquid. Bring to a simmer, whisking constantly until thickened. Sauté mushrooms in a T. of butter and garlic seasoning. Surround the roast with the mushrooms. Sprinkle pepper. Serve with wine sauce. Serves 6.

Liver & Veal Loaf

¾ lbs. pork liver
¾ lbs. ground veal
2 T. melted fat
1 egg, beaten
½ cup catsup
Sliced bacon (optional)
1 tsp. salt
1 tsp. pepper
1 tsp. Worcestershire sauce
1 cup water
1 cup oatmeal (regular or quick cooking type)

Cook pork liver 5 minutes; drain and grind. Combine with all other ingredients except bacon. Pack in greased loaf pan. Cover with slice bacon or brush with melted fat. Bake in a moderately hot oven for 1 hour. Serve hot with gravy or tomato sauce or slice cold.
—Grandmother Rose Begin

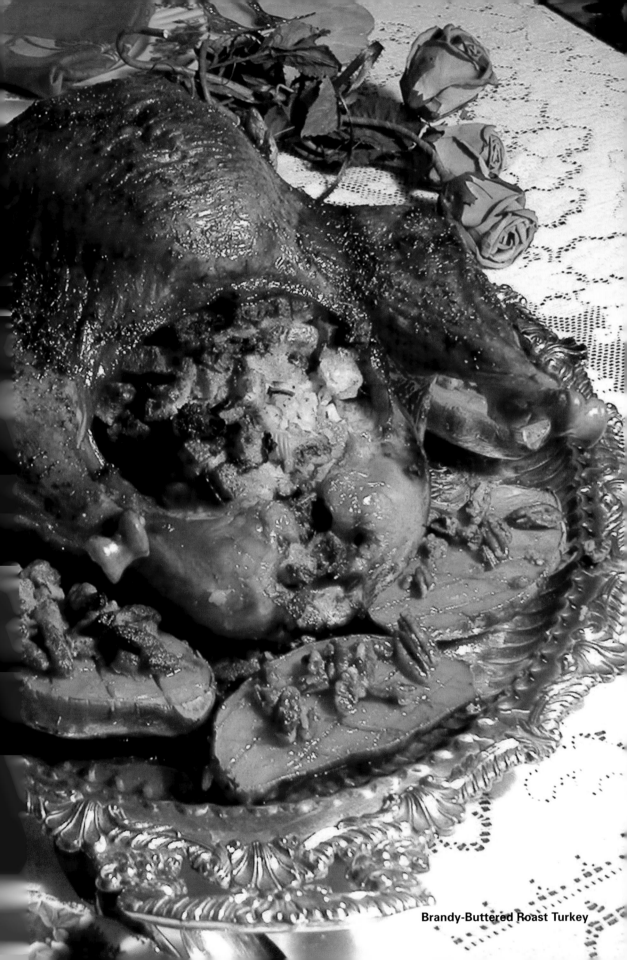

Brandy-Buttered Roast Turkey

Herb-Crusted Prime Rib (RECIPE PG. 50)

Sausage Bread Stuffing

In an 8-quart Dutch oven over medium heat cook 2 (16 oz.) packages of pork sausage meat until browned. With slotted spoon remove pork sausage meat to medium bowl. Set aside.

Pour all but ¼ cup drippings from Dutch oven. In hot drippings over medium heat cook 2 cups diced celery and 1 large diced onion until tender, about 10 minutes stirring occasionally.

Remove Dutch oven from heat; stir in cooked sausage, 16 cups white bread cubes (about 30 slices), 4 eggs slightly beaten, ½ cup milk, ⅓ cup minced parsley, 1 ½ tsp. thyme leaves, 1 tsp. salt, ½ tsp. seasoned pepper and ½ tsp. ground sage. Toss gently to mix well.

Oyster Dressing

½ cup (1 stick) butter
½ cup onion, finely chopped
½ cup celery, finely chopped
½ cup green bell pepper, finely chopped
2 T. minced garlic
1 large bay leaf
Salt and black pepper
Pinch of thyme
1 T. Worcestershire sauce
24 shucked oysters
1 large egg
2 cups seasoned bread crumbs
1 T. parsley, finely chopped

Melt butter in a large skillet and sauté onion, celery, bell pepper and garlic. When vegetables are tender, add bay leaf, thyme, Worcestershire and oysters along with any oyster water. Cook for 2 to 3 minutes until edges of oysters begin to curl. Season mixture with salt and pepper to taste. Working quickly stir in the egg. Fold in bread crumbs and parsley. Cook for 1 to 2 minutes until mixture is heated through. Yields 3 cups.

Cranberry Sauce with Port and Tangerine

1 (12 oz.) bag fresh or frozen cranberries
¾ cup sugar
½ cup ruby Port
3 (3 by ½ inch) strips tangerine zest
⅓ cup tangerine juice (from about 2 tangerines

Bring cranberries, sugar, Port, and zest to a simmer in a small heavy saucepan over medium heat, stirring until sugar has dissolved. Simmer, uncovered, stirring occasionally, until cran-berries burst, about 12 minutes. Remove from heat and stir in juice. Cool completely.

Sauce can be made 1 week ahead and chilled in an airtight container.

Double-baked Roquefort Potatoes

6 (10-12 oz.) russet potatoes, scrubbed
⅔ cup crumbled Roquefort cheese
½ cup sour cream
6 T. freshly grated Parmesan cheese
2 T. (¼ stick) butter, cut into small pieces
Chopped fresh parsley

Preheat oven to 375º. Pierce potatoes with fork. Place potatoes directly on oven rack. Bake until potatoes are tender, about 1 hr. 15 minutes. Transfer to baking sheet. Cool 5 minutes.

Halve each potato lengthwise. Scoop flesh from potatoes leaving ½ inch thick shell; place flesh in large bowl. Add crumbled Roquefort cheese and sour cream to potato flesh. Mash until smooth. Season mixture with salt and pepper.

Spoon potato mixture into 8 potato shells, mounding slightly and dividing equally (reserve remaining 4 potato shells for another use). Place potatoes on baking sheet. Sprinkle Parmesan cheese over potatoes. Dot with butter. This may be made one day ahead. Cover and refrigerate.

Preheat oven to 400º. Bake potatoes until heated through and beginning to brown on top, about 25 minutes. Sprinkle parsley over potatoes and serve.

Old-Fashioned Corn Relish

4 fresh ears of corn or 1 (10 oz.) package frozen whole kernel corn (2 cups)
1/3 cup julienned carrot
1/3 cup sliced green onions or chopped onion
1/3 cup chopped red or green sweet pepper
1/3 cup sugar
1/3 cup cider vinegar
1/2 tsp. salt
1/2 tsp. celery seeds
1/2 tsp. dry mustard
1/4 tsp. bottled hot pepper sauce

Remove husks from fresh ears of corn if using; scrub with a stiff brush to remover silks and rinse. Cut kernels from cob. Cook kernels, covered, in a small amount of boiling salted water for 4 minutes. (Or cook frozen corn according to package directions.) Drain corn. Transfer corn to a medium bowl; stir in carrot, green onions and sweet pepper. Set aside.

In a small saucepan, combine sugar, vinegar, salt, celery seeds, dry mustard, and hot pepper sauce. Bring to boiling; reduce heat. Simmer the sugar mixture uncovered, for 2 minutes. Carefully pour the sugar mixture over corn mixture. Let cool slightly. Cover and chill for at least 4 hours or up to 2 weeks.

Serve with a slotted spoon, if you like, with pork, beef or poultry. Makes about 3 cups (twelve 1/4 cup servings.)

Sweet Potato Fries

Peel potatoes. Cut into thin strips. Toss in olive oil and Kosher salt. Bake at 400º until crisp.

Creamy Rice Pudding

1/2 cup rice
3 cups boiling water
1 tsp. salt
3/4 cups sweetened condensed milk
2 eggs, well beaten
1/2 cup raisins
1/4 tsp. nutmeg
1 tsp. vanilla

Wash rice, add water and salt, cook covered in a double boiler about 40 minutes or until rice is tender. Add milk, eggs, and raisins. Flavor with nutmeg and vanilla. Cook 10 minutes longer. —*Grandmother Rose Begin*

Angel Erdman's Ribbon Gelatin

5 boxes (3 oz. each) gelatin, in varying flavors
Boiling water
2 envelopes unflavored gelatin
1 cup water
2 cups coffee cream
1 cup sugar
1/2 tsp. salt
2 cups sour cream

Separately mix each box of gelatin with 1 1/4 cups of boiling water.

To make filling, mix the unflavored gelatin with 1 cup water, coffee cream, sugar and salt. Cook on medium heat until sugar is dissolved. Cool. Add the sour cream and mix until smooth.

In a dish, 9x13 inches, alternate layers of gelatin with filling. Let each layer of gelatin set until firm before spreading with filling. Let filling set before adding next layer of gelatin. Continue until you end up with a layer of gelatin. Makes about 16 servings.

Bananas Foster Shortcake

BISCUITS:

3 ½ cups all-purpose flour
2 ½ T. baking powder
1 ½ tsp. baking soda
5 T. sugar
¾ tsp. cinnamon
1 stick plus 3 tsp. butter, cut into bits and chilled, plus melted butter for brushing the biscuits
½ cup chopped banana
⅔ cup buttermilk

Preheat oven to 400º and line a baking sheet with parchment paper. In a large bowl, whisk together flour, baking powder, baking soda, 4 T. plus 1 tsp. sugar and ½ tsp. cinnamon. Blend in chilled butter until mixture resembles coarse meal and blend in banana. Add buttermilk and gently stir until a dough just forms.

On a lightly floured surface gently knead dough 3 times and press into a 1 ¼ inch thick round. Cut out 4 biscuits with a 3-inch round cutter and transfer to prepared baking sheet.

In a small bowl whisk together remaining 2 tsp. sugar and remaining ¼ tsp. cinnamon. Brush biscuits with some melted butter and sprinkle with cinnamon sugar. Bake biscuits in middle of oven 15-20 minutes or until golden brown. Brush biscuits with more melted butter and cool on baking sheet. Halve biscuits.

SAUCE:

1 cup heavy cream
½ cup plus 2 T. firmly packed dark brown sugar
1 T. banana liquer
¼ tsp. cinnamon
4 bananas
½ cup heavy cream, whipped

In a saucepan cook heavy cream over high heat until reduced to about ½ cup. Remove pan from heat and stir in sugar, stirring until dissolved. Stir in liqueur and cinnamon.

Arrange a biscuit half on each of 4 dessert plates and slice a banana onto it. Pour sauce over bananas and top with a dollop of whipped cream. Arrange remaining biscuit halves on top of cream. Serves 4.

Elaine's Pie Crust

1 ½ cups flour
1 tsp. sugar
½ tsp. salt
⅓ cup fresh cold beer
⅓ cup chilled lard

Stir together flour, sugar and salt. With pastry blender or two knives, cut lard into flour until mixture resembles cornmeal. With fork, mix in beer gradually until evenly moistened. Mold dough into ball. Refrigerate several hours. Roll out in a circle to fit a 10-inch pie plate. Makes a single 10-inch crust.

Grand Marnier Baked Custard

2 cups heavy cream
6 egg yolks
1 ½ cups milk
3 whole eggs
3-4 strips orange peel (colored part only)
½ cup sugar
2 T. Grand Marnier

Preheat oven to 325º. In a heavy saucepan, combine cream, milk, and orange peel. Bring to a boil, remove from heat and let cool for 10 minutes. Remove and discard orange peel. In a large bowl, combine egg yolks, whole eggs and sugar. Beat until a light lemon color; then add cream mixture and Grand Marnier. Pour into custard cups and place in a baking pan. Add boiling water to pan to come ⅔ up sides of cups. Place aluminum foil over top and bake for 40-45 minutes until center of custard is just set. A knife blade inserted into center of custard should come out clean.

VIP Pecan Pie

1 cup pecan halves
¼ cup Southern Comfort
1 cup brown sugar (packed)
2 T. flour
1 T. butter or margarine
1 cup dark brown syrup
3 eggs, beaten
¼ tsp. salt
1 prepared pastry

Toss pecans and whiskey until pecans are coated. Let stand 1 hour or until most of the whiskey is absorbed. Heat oven to 325º. Mix brown sugar and flour; beat in softened butter until creamy. Beat in corn syrup, eggs and salt. Stir in pecans and whiskey.

Turn pecan mixture into pastry-lined pie pan. Cover edge with 2-3-inch strip of aluminum foil to prevent excessive browning; remove foil last 15 minutes of baking. Bake until center is set (about 1 hour and 10 minutes). Serve with flavored whipped cream, if desired. –*Jacquie Begin*

NOTE: Regular bourbon whiskey may be used instead of Southern Comfort.

Sanders Refrigerator Rolls

1 cup shortening
1 cup sugar
1 cup mashed potatoes
1 quart milk
1 envelope active dry yeast
10 to 12 cups flour
2 tsp. salt
2 tsp. baking powder
1 tsp. baking powder

In large mixer bowl, cream shortening and sugar until light and fluffy. Add potatoes and continue creaming until well mixed. Heat milk to lukewarm. Dissolve yeast in milk, then pour until creamed mixture. Add enough flour to make cake-like batter (about

4 cups). Stir in salt. Cover and let rise in a warm, draft-free place for 2 hours.

With wooden spoon, stir in enough remaining flour (6 to 8 cups), baking powder and soda to form a soft dough. Turn out on floured surface and knead until smooth and elastic (10-15 minutes). Place in a large greased bowl, turn to grease top, cover and chill at least 30 minutes.

Shape as much as needed for one ball (about 1 ½ inches in diameter) or as desired. Place about 2 inches apart in greased pan. Let rise in warm, draft-free place until doubled (60-70 minutes). Bake in preheated 450º oven for 15 minutes or until golden brown on top. Cover remaining dough and chill until ready to use. Keeps 5 to 6 days. Makes 8 to 9 dozen rolls, depending on size.

Sanders Coffee Cake & Streusel Topping

3 pkgs. dry yeast
1 cup warm water
1 T. sugar
¾ lbs. butter
1 ½ cups buttermilk
8 oz. sour cream
6 large eggs, beaten
1 T. salt
1 T. vanilla
2 cups granulated sugar
5 lbs. flour minus one cup

COFFEE CAKE:
Sprinkle yeast over warm water. Stir in 1 T. sugar. Let stand 5 minutes until bubbly (in small bowl). Melt butter and combine it with buttermilk, sour cream and eggs. Add salt and vanilla.

Meanwhile, place bubbled yeast mixture in 6-8 quart kettle or roomy bowl and stir in 2 cups sugar with 2 cups flour. Alternately add egg mixture with half of remaining flour, then work in rest of flour one cup at a time until it can be kneaded into an elastic and

smooth ball. Toss dough on lightly floured surface, kneading 10 minutes. Place in plastic bag that permits it to double in bulk while refrigerated overnight.

Ninety minutes before baking, divide dough into five equal portions. Knead each with about 3 to 4 T. flour. Shape into balls and place each one in a greased 8 or 9-inch layer pan. Sprinkle with streusel topping. Let rise until doubled (about 1 ¼ hour). Bake at 350º about 30 to 35 minutes. Let cool in pans one hour before cutting or freezing. Makes 5 cakes.

STREUSEL TOPPING:
1 stick butter
1 T. cinnamon
½ cup sugar
⅛ tsp. salt
½ cup flour
1 cup chopped walnuts or raisins (optional)
Melt butter and stir in remaining ingredients until crumbly. Sprinkle on coffee cake dough as directed.

Note: Make coffee cake bread instead by shaping dough into 5 loaves and letting it rise in buttered 9-inch bread loaf pans. Streusel mixture may be sprinkle on top or spread between 2 layers of the dough to be used in each pan. Let rise until doubled, then bake at 350º for 30 to 35 minutes.

Sanders Butter Frosting
1 stick plus 6 T. butter or margarine
1 cup sugar

Beat at least 15 minutes. Gradually add ¾ cup milk just barely warm, and 1 tsp. flavoring.

Sanders Glossy Chocolate Fudge Icing
½ cup vegetable oil
1 cup cocoa
½ tsp. salt
½ T. vanilla extract
2 ½ cups brown sugar
½ cup maple sugar
¼ cup melted dark Baker's chocolate
⅔ cup evaporated milk
Heat oil to approximately 200º. Turn off heat, add cocoa and stir well. Add chocolate, mix to a smooth paste. Allow to cool to 100º. In the meantime, place milk in mixing bowl and heat over hot water to lukewarm 120º. Add salt, vanilla, and brown sugar. Mix at low speed and when sugar is dissolved, add maple syrup. Add above cooled chocolate past and mix slowly until smooth. Use immediately to frost cake.

FOR CREAMY FUDGE ICING:
Place 3 cups Glossy Chocolate Fudge Icing and 1 cup sweet butter or margarine in mixing bowl. Mix at medium speed until creamy or fluffy.

Sanders Hot Fudge Topping
⅓ cup white milk
½ lb. Sanders Milk Chocolate
½ pint Sanders vanilla ice cream or 1 cup soft ice cream
1 lb. caramels
1 tsp. vanilla extract

Place milk and caramels in double boiler. Heat and stir until hot, smooth cream is obtained. Chop chocolate and add to the above hot cream. Stir until melted. Mix in soft ice cream and vanilla extract and stir until smooth.

VARIATION:
Instead of using whole milk, substitute ⅓ cup very strong coffee.

THIS PAGE: **The house on Dunn Dr.** OPPOSITE: **First Holy Communion with Godmother Frances**

1980-1993

THE DUNN DRIVE YEARS

Robert built a beautiful home on the Grand Traverse Bay. What could I say? I loved it. My main job was Marie-Chantal—sewing dresses (I have three boxes) ballet, piano, birthdays, Halloween parties and Christmas celebrations.

In 1983 we lived in Europe for nine months touring, studying wine, getting ideas for the Chateau Winery. We returned in November, bought a 60 acre cherry farm and my once handsome, debonair, French CEO became a farmer. Tuxedos, dark suits and ties flash across my mind. I see dusty boots, holes in trousers and pockets and a smile from ear to ear!

The land was prepared. In 1986 the first 10 acres of grapes were planted by friends and neighbors. Houses are sold easier than memories. In 1993 that's what we did and moved to 15900 Rue de Vin.

"I will give thanks to the Lord with all my heart."–PSALM 111:1-2

Robert focused on the grapes. What is more meaningful? At the Last Supper, Jesus took wine and changed it to His blood. Wine is biblical.

"I am the vine, you are the branches. He who abides in Me, and I in Him, bears much fruit; for without Me you can do nothing." –JOHN 15

Wine is romance.

THIS PAGE: **Joseph** OPPOSITE: **When Elaine married Joe, I knew she was the one—a truly beautiful lady. Loving and losing him made us friends forever.**

"By the miracle of His life in us and with us, we will realize our greatest achievements."

It was early spring 1988 when my dearest brother Joseph was diagnosed with lung cancer. How could it be? He was extremely health-conscious— did not smoke, bicycled, ran, — all types of exercise. For six months we all prayed and tried to remain positive. However, on October 22 we received the news that the end was near. Joseph met Jesus on October 23, 1988.

My pain and sorrow was so intense that I just lay on my bed and uncontrollably cried my heart out. When I arose I saw this bright star fall from the heavens. To my amazement it landed right on my windowsill, paused, and then went straight to Heaven. Yes, Joseph continues to look after me even today. I pray to him, "Joe, take care of me."

"Pruning is how God answers your prayers that your life will please Him more and have greater impact for Eternity."

Our beautiful home on the Bay provided us with many opportunities to celebrate life and rejoice in the "Wonders of His Love." Fun-filled birthdays, Halloween with a new costume every year, glorious Christmases along with a wonderful Seminary Reunion enlivened our lives with exuberant entertainment.

During the span of these thirteen years, we renewed many old and made many new friendships. It was during this time that Marie-Chantal found out who Santa Claus really was. As I

THIS PAGE: Robert on first planting day at Chateau Chantal OPPOSITE: King Robert, Queen Nadine and Princess Chantal

was driving her and a friend, I heard her say, "Santa ripped off his beard and there was Dad."

Her piano birthday cake became an annual request. With an abundance of free time, I started cooking on the weekends at the Traverse Manor, an assisted living place. The residents liked my spicy food and desserts. I always seem to have fun wherever I go, but the kiss from Oliver in the kitchen was something else.

The Next Time Around

Lord, in my next life I would like to be a vineyard worker. Not in the traditional Christian sense of one whoe does your work, but in the everyday sense, as one who tills the ground, prunes the vines, gathers the grapes, and looks upon quiet sunsets. I know it seems less important than being a minister or a professor, but, Lord, doesn't the world need grapes and jellies and vintage wines as well as sermons and lectures, books and papers?

I want to be quiet in my next life, Lord, and listen for you in the growing sounds of the grapes, in the gentle winds and rains, in the groaning of the earth as it lovingly gives birth to crops. I want to see you in the clean fields, the neat rows of stakes and vines, the barns and vats and cellars and bottles. I want to walk softly among the rows, conscious of the holiness of the soil. I want to caress the clusters into ripeness, and pick them at just the proper moment, not a day too soon or a day too late. I want to feel you in the noonday heat rising from the earth like a thermal tide, and in the evening cool that makes my skin tingle when born on a little breeze. And I don't want any money, Lord, only my daily Bread. And I don't want to own the vineyard. All I want to do is work from day to day and feel the tiredness of my body like a benediction when day is done. I want to know the wonder of life like a simple man or child, and enjoy the splendor of the world for ways in which I've been too busy, this time around. Even if I don't make it, Lord, it's a good dream and it enriches my life now. For that I am grateful, and I pray a blessing on every real vineyard worker, who may be wishing he were in my job and not in his own. Amen.

–JOHN KILLINGER

1980-1993

RECIPES

APPETIZERS & SOUPS
Artichoke Dip
Smoked Whitefish Dip
Lavash Cracker Bread
Smoked Whitefish Cheesecake
Lobster Bisque
Country Style Italian Winter Soup

MAIN DISHES
Seared Bourbon Street Steaks
Golden Garlic Mustard Sauce
Pan Seared Filet Mignon with Roasted
  Potatoes
Merlot Sauce
Strip Steak or Tenderloin
Sticky Spicy Ribs
Savory Meatloaf
Broiled Marinated Chuck Steak
Roast Duck with Cherry Wine Sauce

FISH DISHES
Steamed Mussels
Shrimp Risotto with Orange and Grand
  Marnier
Cold Poached Salmon with Mustard
  Lime Sauce
Quick Nutty Salmon
Steamed Salmon
Blackened Fish
Crab Cakes

SAUCES
Creamy Horseradish Dressing
Horseradish Mayonnaise
Sour Cream and Horseradish
Lemon-Butter Sauce
Creole Sauce
Pesto
Sweet-Sour Sauce
20 Minute Spaghetti Sauce
Balsamic Vinaigrette

SIDE DISHES
Mediterranean Onion Relish
Bread & Butter Pickles

DESSERTS
Lindsey's Pie Crust
Perfect Nut Crust
Cheesecake Brulee
Lacy Dessert Baskets
Cannoli
Chocolate Steamed Pudding
Pistachio Whiskey Cake
Cream Cheese Whiskey Frosting
Orleans Apple Torte
Mountain-High Key Lime Pie
Marie-Chantal's Keyboard
  Birthday Cake

Lobster Bisque (RECIPE PG. 69)

Artichoke Dip

1 cup Miracle Whip or Miracle Whip Light
  Dressing
1 cup sour cream
2 cans (14 oz.) artichoke hearts, drained,
  chopped
1 cup (4 oz.) Kraft 100% Grated Parmesan
  Cheese
8 oz. pkg. softened cream cheese
1 clove garlic, minced
Chopped tomato
Sliced green onions

Mix all ingredients except tomato and
onions. Spoon into 9-inch pie plate or quiche
dish. Bake at 350º for 20 to 25 minutes or
until lightly browned. Sprinkle with tomato
and onions, if desired. Serve with crackers.
Makes 3 ½ cups.

TO MAKE AHEAD:
Prepare dip as directed except for baking;
cover. Refrigerate overnight. When ready to
serve, bake, uncovered, at 350º for 20 to 25
minutes or until lightly browned.

Smoked Whitefish Dip

4 oz. cream cheese, room temperature
¼ cup sour cream
1 medium size smoked whitefish, deboned
1 dash hot sauce
1 pinch cayenne pepper
¼ tsp. salt
¼ sweet onion, finely minced
1 tsp. fresh garlic, minced
½ tsp. Dijon mustard
1 T. olive oil

Combine all ingredients in blender and blend
until smooth. To serve hot, spread in an 8
oz. baking dish and bake at 350º for approximately 30 minutes, or until warm in the middle and golden on top. Serve with warm
bread or sesame crackers.

Lavash Cracker Bread

1 ½ cups unbleached white flour
½ cup organic whole wheat flour
1 tsp. salt
1 envelope active dry yeast
2 T. olive oil
½ tsp. granulated sugar
⅔ cup warm water
5 T. sesame seeds

Combine flour, salt, yeast, and 3 T. sesame
seeds in a large bowl. Mix together olive oil,
sugar and warm water and slowly add to dry
ingredients, stirring constantly. Knead dough
until it is smooth and elastic. Shape into a
ball and rub oil over the entire surface. Place
dough in a bowl and cover the bowl with
plastic wrap or aluminum foil. Place a hot,
damp towel over the covered bowl and let
dough rise until doubled in bulk, 1 to 2
hours.

Punch dough down and in 2 pieces. Roll
out as thinly possible. Sprinkle the remaining
sesame seeds and roll again. Transfer dough
to baking sheet. It is important for the
dough to be evenly pressed and very thin.
Score into free hand pieces. Bake at 400º for
about 8 minutes watching closely. While
Lavash is baking, repeat the process with the
second piece.

To serve, break Lavash into pieces. Makes
about 30 crackers. Serve with brie, assorted
cheeses and grapes.

Smoked Whitefish Cheesecake

CRUST:
2 T. butter
¾ cup fresh bread crumbs
½ cup freshly grated Parmesan cheese
½ tsp. fresh dill

FILLING:
4 ½ T. butter
2 ½ lbs. cream cheese, softened
6 eggs
¾ cup grated soft white cheese
¾ lb. smoked whitefish, skinned and boned
½ cup half and half
½ tsp. salt
½ tsp. white pepper
¾ cup chopped onion, sautéed until soft

Blend all the crust ingredients in a blender or food processor and sprinkle into a 10-inch springform pan. Preheat oven to 325º. In a food processor, blend together butter, cream cheese, eggs, white cheese, half and half, salt, and pepper. When thoroughly blended, add the onion and smoked whitefish.

Pour batter into the prepared pan and wrap the bottom with aluminum foil. Place pan into a larger pan with enough hot water to come halfway up the sides of the pan. Bake for approximately 1 ½ hours. Then turn off the oven and let stand for another hour. Chill well before slicing.

Lobster Bisque

2 lbs. cooked lobster tails with shells intact
4 carrots, cut in 1-inch pieces (2 cups)
½ lb. potatoes, peeled and cut in 1-inch cubes (1 ½ cups)
2 small leeks (white part only), thinly sliced (1 cup)
2 stalks celery, sliced (1 cup)
1 bay leaf
½ tsp. peppercorns
2 cups chicken stock
3 T. unsalted butter
2 T. all-purpose flour
2 cups milk
½ cup heavy cream
1 cup Chardonnay
1 T. Lobster Minor's Lobster Base
Fresh chives and paprika for garnish

Split each lobster in half lengthwise. Remove intestinal vein in tail section. Remove lobster meat from shells, reserving shells. Discard content of body section and rinse out shell. Finely chop meat. Wrap and refrigerate. Crack shells.

In large pot, combine cracked lobster shells, carrots, potatoes, leeks, celery, bay leaf, and peppercorns. Pour in stock. Bring to boiling. Reduce heat. Cover and simmer for 25 to 35 minutes until vegetables are tender.

Discard lobster shells. Pureé vegetables with broth.

In another large saucepan, melt butter over medium heat. Stir in flour and 1 T. Lobster Minor's Lobster Base. Cook, stirring constantly until mixture starts to brown. Whisk in milk. Cook, stirring constantly, until mixture thickens and boils.

Reduce heat to low. Stir in pureed vegetables, reserved lobster meat, cream and wine. Heat gently, stirring occasionally until just heated through. DO NOT boil. Season to taste with salt and pepper.

Country Style Italian Winter Soup

Country Style Italian Winter Soup

Sauté:

4 Italian sausages, halved and sliced
1 boned chicken breast sliced in 1 ½ inch slivers
1 T. garlic
2 T. olive oil

Add:

6 knob onions
3 zucchini, sliced
12 oz. mushrooms, sliced
1 pkg. frozen spinach, chopped

Cook until tender.

In a large pot combine:

1 cup brown rice
1 cup lentils
3 T. Jamison's Chicken Soup base
water to cover

Cook until tender and add above ingredients.
Season with oregano, thyme and basil.
Before serving add grated lemon rind,
fresh grated Parmesan cheese and cider vinegar.—*Helene Matecki*

Seared Bourbon Street Steaks

2 Sterling Silver tenderloin steaks (1 ½ inches thick)
2 T. Bourbon
2 tsp. brown sugar
⅛ tsp. ground black pepper
Golden Garlic Mustard Sauce

Combine Bourbon, brown sugar and pepper;
rub over steaks. Preheat grill to medium. Place
steaks on grid over medium coals. Grill 13 to
17 minutes for rare (140º) to medium (160º)
turning once halfway through cooking time.
Season to taste with salt and pepper. Serve
steaks with Golden Garlic Mustard Sauce.

Golden Garlic Mustard Sauce

¼ cup mayonnaise
¼ cup sour cream
2 T. grainy mustard
1 T. chopped fresh chives
½ tsp. grated orange rind
½ tsp. minced garlic
¼ tsp. salt
¼ tsp. Cayenne pepper

Combine all ingredients in a small bowl.
Cover and refrigerate until ready to use.
Makes about ⅔ cup. Serves 2.

Pan-seared Filet Mignon with Roasted Potatoes and Merlot Sauce

4 large russet (baking) potatoes (about 2 lbs. total)
About ¼ cup vegetable oil
Six 1 ¼-inch thick filets mignon (about 3 lbs. total)
About 2 cups Merlot sauce

Preheat oven to 425º and oil 2 baking sheets.
Cut potatoes lengthwise into ½ inch-thick
slices and arrange in one layer on baking
sheets. Lightly brush slices with some oil and
season with salt and pepper. Roast potatoes
in middle and lower thirds of oven until
golden brown and tender, about 35 minutes,
and keep warm.

Pat filets mignon dry and season with salt
and pepper. In a large heavy skillet heat 2 T.
oil over moderately high heat until hot but not
smoking and brown filets on both sides, without crowding, about 5 minutes total. Transfer
filets to a shallow baking pan and roast in
middle of oven about 7 minutes for medium-rare. On each of 6 plates fan 3 potato slices
and top with a filet. Drizzle filets with some
sauce. Serve remaining sauce on the side.
Serves 6. *Merlot Sauce recipe on page 70.*

Merlot Sauce

¼ cup water
¼ cup sugar
3 T. red-wine vinegar
1 cup finely chopped onion (about 1 medium)
3 T. unsalted butter
2 cups Merlot or other dry red wine
2 cups rich veal stock

In a small heavy saucepan bring water with sugar to a boil, stirring until sugar is dissolved. Boil syrup, without stirring, until a golden caramel. Remove pan from heat and carefully add vinegar down side of pan (caramel will steam and harden). Cook caramel over moderate heat, stirring, until dissolved, about 3 minutes and remove from heat.

In a heavy saucepan cook onion in butter over moderate heat, stirring, until golden, about 5 minutes. Stir in wine and boil until mixture is reduced to about 1 cup, about 15 minutes. Stir in stock and boil until mixture is reduced to about 2 cups, about 10 minutes. Remove pan from heat and stir in caramel. Pour sauce through a sieve into a bowl.

Sauce may be made 2 days ahead, cooled completely, and chilled, covered. Reheat sauce before serving.

Strip Steak or Tenderloin

Marinate meat (about 2 hours) in:
2 T. Onion Soup Mix
1 T. Bisto
2 T. Worcestershire sauce
1 T. Instant Espresso
1 T. coarsely cracked peppercorn
2 T. red wine

Grill or preheat broiler. Place steak on rack in broiling pan (reserving marinade). Broil about 3-5 inches from heat; 5 minutes on each side or desired doneness, brushing frequently with marinade. Garnish with mushrooms sautéed in butter.

Sticky Spicy Ribs

FOR RIBS:
2 T. packed dark brown sugar
1 ½ tsp. salt
2 T. paprika (not hot)
1 ½ tsp. Blackening Seasoning
1 ½ tsp. Instant Espresso coffee
1 ½ tsp. ground cumin
1 tsp. ground allspice
½ tsp. black pepper
2 (2 lb.) racks baby back ribs

FOR SAUCE:
1 ½ cups chopped onion (from 1 large)
6 garlic cloves, finely chopped
Cajun seasoning
2 T. vegetable oil
1 ½ cups ketchup
½ cup cider vinegar
6 T. soy sauce
½ cup water
¼ cup packed dark brown sugar
1 ½ tsp. salt
¾ tsp. black pepper

Whisk together brown sugar, salt, spices, and coffee in a small bowl. Line a 17x12x1-inch heavy-duty baking pan with a double layer of foil, then oil foil. Pat ribs dry and arrange in baking pan. Rub ribs all over with spice mixture and marinate, meaty sides up, covered and chilled for 2 ½ hours. Bring ribs to room temperature, about 30 minutes. Put oven rack in middle position and preheat oven to 350º. Cover pan tightly with foil; bake 1 ¼ hours. Remove foil.

Make sauce while ribs bake: Cook onion, garlic, in oil in a 2-quart heavy saucepan over moderate heat, stirring occasionally, until softened, about 6 minutes. Add remaining ingredients and simmer, uncovered, stirring occasionally, 15 minutes. Pureé sauce in 2 or 3 batches in a blender until smooth (use caution when blending hot liquids). Set aside 1 cup sauce for serving with ribs.

Grill ribs: Brush ribs with remaining sauce and with medium-hot charcoal (moderate heat for gas. Grill until sauce is carmelized & slightly blackened.

Savory Meatloaf

3 T. vegetable oil
1 cup onions, finely chopped
1 cup celery, finely chopped
1 lb. ground sirloin steak
½ lb. ground veal
½ lb. ground pork
2 eggs, lightly beaten
1 tsp. powdered sage
1 tsp. dried thyme
½ cup chopped fresh parsley
½ cup seltzer water
Salt and freshly ground pepper
1 ½ cups Herb-flavored Pepperidge
  Farm Stuffing, finely ground

SAUCE:

1 cup tomato sauce
2 T. dark brown sugar
2 T. soy sauce
1 medium onion, thinly sliced and separated into rings

Preheat oven to 400º. In a medium-sized skillet, heat oil. Add onions and celery, and cook until softened but not brown, 7-8 minutes. Remove from heat and let cool. In a large bowl, combine ground beef, veal, pork, stuffing crumbs, eggs, sage, thyme, parsley, seltzer, cooked onions and celery. Mix thoroughly with your hands until all ingredients are blended and mixture is light and spongy. Add salt and pepper to taste. Mound into a loaf on a lightly oiled shallow baking pan.

SAUCE:

Mix together tomato sauce, brown sugar, and soy sauce. Spread half the sauce over entire surface of meatloaf, and arrange onion rings over all. Bake for 30 minutes. Remove from oven, cover loaf with remaining sauce and return to oven. Reduce heat to 375º and bake 30 minutes longer. Serve hot, warm, or at room temperature. Serves 6-8.

Broiled Marinated Chuck Steak

1 (1 ½ -inch thick) beef chuck blade steak
  (about 2 ½ to 3 lbs.)
¾ cup soy sauce
¼ cup white vinegar
3 T. Worcestershire
¼ cup packed brown sugar
2 T. salad oil
1 tsp. ground ginger
Parsley for garnish

About 5 hours before serving or early in the day: On a cutting board with sharp knife, trim excess fat from chuck steak. In 13x9-inch baking dish, combine soy sauce with remaining ingredients except parsley. Add steak and turn to coat with marinade. Cover and let meat marinate in refrigerator about 4 hours, turning meat occasionally.

About 1 hour before serving: Preheat broiler. Place steak on rack in broiling pan (reserving marinade). Broil steak about 3-5 inches from source of heat, 30 minutes for rare or until desired doneness, brushing frequently with marinade and turning meat once. Place steak on cutting boards; garnish with parsley. Makes 6 servings.

Roast Duck with Cherry-Wine Sauce

1 duck (about 4 lbs.) thawed, if frozen, giblets and neck removed
½ tsp. salt
½ tsp. pepper
1 (8 oz.) jar cherry jam
½ cup chicken broth
½ cup dry red wine

Rub duck cavity with salt and pepper; close with skewers. Fasten neck skin and wings to back; tie legs close to body. Place on rack in shallow roasting pan. Roast in 350º oven 1 to 1 ½ hours, draining off fat as it accumulates. Remove from oven; cool slightly. Mix jam, broth and wine; set aside.

Remove skewers and string; cut duck in half. Place cut sides down in clean roasting pan or oven-proof serving dish. Pour half the sauce over duck; return to oven. Roast 30 minutes longer or until drumstick feels tender when pressed, basting with remaining sauce several times. Remove to serving platter, spoon sauce on top. Makes 4 servings.

Steamed Mussels

2 T. unsalted butter or extra-virgin oil
1 bay leaf
6 shallots, minced
1 tsp. white peppercorns, crushed
4 garlic cloves, minced
2 fresh thyme sprigs
1 celery stalk, peeled and finely diced
1 large bunch flat-leaf (Italian) parsley stemmed and minced (about ½ cup)
2 cups dry white wine
4 lbs. mussels, scrubbed and debearded
½ cup heavy cream

In a stockpot, melt butter or olive oil over medium heat and saute shallots and peppercorns for 2 minutes. Add garlic and celery and sauté for about 1 minute. Stir in half parsley, bay leaf, and thyme. Add white wine and cook to reduce it by half.

Add mussels and cream, cover, and cook, stirring occasionally, for 4 to 5 minutes, or until mussels have opened. Using a slotted spoon, transfer mussels to a deep serving dish. Discard any mussels that are not opened. Cover dish to keep mussels warm.

Cook mussel pan juices until reduced by half. Add remaining parsley and pour sauce over the mussels. *To serve:* Place a dish of mussels in the center of the table and let guests serve themselves, or divide mussels among individual deep bowls.

Shrimp Risotto with Orange and Grand Marnier

20 large shrimps, peeled and deveined
¾ tsp. salt
¾ tsp. white pepper
2 T. light olive oil
2 T. butter
⅓ cup finely minced onion
1 ½ cups rice
5 ½ cups hot chicken or shrimp stock
1 cup orange juice
2 T. Grand Marnier
2 T. light cream
¼ cup grated Parmesan cheese
1 T. chopped capers

Season shrimp with 1 T. olive oil and ¼ tsp. each salt & pepper. Heat butter and olive oil over medium heat in a large, cast-iron skillet. Add onion and cook until it is translucent. Add rice and stir to coat well. Add 1 cup of stock and cook, stirring until it is absorbed. Continue to stir in stock, 1 cup at a time.

After the 4th cup is added, put an 8-inch skillet on moderate heat. When skillet is hot, add shrimp and cook until cooked through, about 3 minutes. Remove shrimp to a dish and cover. Add remaining stock to shrimp skillet. Bring to a boil and stir in rice. When stock is almost absorbed, add orange juice, Grand Marnier, salt & pepper. (Rice should absorb all of the liquid.) Stir in light cream, Parmesan, capers and shrimp. Serve each bowl of risotto with 5 pieces of shrimp. Garnish with Italian parsley, if desired. Serves 4.

Steamed Mussels

Quick Nutty Salmon

Cold Poached Salmon with Mustard-Lime Sauce

6 cups water
2 ½ cups dry white wine
6 (7 to 8 oz.) center cut salmon fillets, skinned
Ground white pepper

SAUCE:
1 cup sour cream
6 T. Dijon mustard
4 tsp. fresh lime juice
4 tsp. honey
1 tsp. grated lime peel
Fresh basil, finely sliced

Pour 3 cups water and 1 ¼ cups wine into each of 2 large skillets and bring to a boil. Turn off heat. Season salmon with salt and white pepper. Place 3 fillets in each skillet; let stand for 6 minutes. Turn salmon over in liquid; let stand 5 minutes. Bring liquid in skillets just to simmer and cook until salmon is just cooked through, about 30 seconds. Using a slotted spatula, transfer salmon to platter. Cover and refrigerate until cold, about 3 hours or up to 1 day. Let salmon stand at room temperature 1 hour before serving.

Stir sour cream, mustard, lime juice, honey and lime peel in bowl to blend. Cover; chill until cold, at least 1 hour. May be made one day ahead. Keep chilled. Arrange salmon on plates. Drizzle with some sauce. Top with basil. Serve, passing sauce separately. Serves 6.

Quick Nutty Salmon

¾ lbs. salmon fillet
1 T. Dijon mustard
Black pepper to taste
1 T. olive oil
¼ cup finely chopped pecans

Combine mustard and olive oil. Spread over fish. Season with pepper and sprinkle pecans. Bake at 450º for 15 minutes or until fish flakes easily. Can also be grilled. *—Ann Hengesbach*

Steamed Salmon

1 (2 lbs.) skinless, boneless salmon fillet
Salt to taste, if desired
Freshly ground pepper to taste
Horseradish mayonnaise, optional

Cut salmon crosswise into 6 portions of equal size. Sprinkle with salt and pepper. Bring water to a boil in the bottom of a steamer. Arrange salmon pieces, skinned, side down on a steamer rack. Place rack on top of steamer bottom. Cover and steam 4 minutes. Remove from heat and let stand 4 minutes longer.

Fish may be served hot with a simple melted butter and lemon sauce, or serve cold with horseradish mayonnaise. Makes 6 servings.

Blackened Fish

½ tsp. onion powder
½ tsp. garlic salt
½ tsp. ground red pepper
½ tsp. dried white pepper
1 T. Blackening Seasoning (Mill House)
4 fish fillets such as cod, catfish, orange roughy, pollock, haddock, whitefish
¼ tsp. pepper
⅛ tsp. ground sage
¼ cup butter or margarine, melted
¼ tsp. dried thyme, crushed

Combine spices. Brush fish with butter; coat with spices (use as much to taste). Preheat cast-iron skillet until drip of water sizzles (about 5 minutes). Add fillets and drizzle about 2 T. butter over fish. Cook about 2 ½ to 3 minutes or until blackened. Turn and drizzle with more butter. Cook about 2 ½ minutes more until fish flakes.

Crab Cakes

1 T. finely chopped scallion
1 T. finely chopped red bell pepper
1 tsp. fresh lemon juice
1 tsp. minced garlic
1 ¼ sticks (5 oz.) unsalted butter, melted
2 T. all purpose flour
¾ cup heavy cream
1 large egg yolk, lightly beaten
2 T. finely chopped fresh basil
1 T. Dijon mustard
1 tsp. salt
8 slices firm whole-wheat sandwich bread,
   cut into 1-inch pieces
¼ cup finely chopped fresh chives
¼ cup finely chopped fresh parsley
1 tsp. black pepper
2 lbs. jumbo lump crabmeat, picked over

Put oven rack in middle position and preheat oven to 425º. Cook scallion, bell pepper, and garlic in 2 T. butter in a 1-quart heavy saucepan over moderate heat, stirring, 1 minute, then whisk in flour and cook roux, stirring constantly, 1 minute. Add cream and bring to a boil, whisking. Reduce heat and simmer, whisking, 2 minutes. (Mixture will be thick.)

Remove from heat and whisk 1 minute, then whisk in yolk, basil, mustard, chile sauce, lemon juice, salt, and chill, uncovered, until cooled, about 15 minutes. While sauce is cooling, line a tray with wax paper. Butter a shallow baking pan. Pulse bread, chives, parsley, and pepper in a food processor until finely chopped and transfer mixture to a plate. Stir crabmeat into sauce and form into 12 (3-inch) patties, arranging them on a tray.

Gently coat each crab cake with crumb mixture and place in baking pan. Drizzle with remaining melted butter and bake until golden and hot, 8 to 10 minutes.

Creamy Horseradish Dressing

¼ cup drained bottled horseradish
1 cup mayonnaise
½ cup sour cream
1 T. fresh lemon juice
1 ½ tsp Dijon-style mustard
1 ½ tsp. Worcestershire sauce
⅛ tsp. salt
¼ tsp. freshly ground pepper
A drop of Tabasco
1 tsp. poppy seeds

In a bowl whisk together the horseradish, mayonnaise, and sour cream until the mixture is combined well. Stir in lemon juice, mustard, Worcestershire sauce, salt, pepper, Tabasco, poppy seeds, and 2 T. water and in a jar with a tight-fitting lid. Chill.

Horseradish Mayonnaise

1 egg yolk
1 T. Dijon mustard
1 T. white vinegar
Salt to taste, if desired
Freshly ground pepper to taste
1 cup corn, peanut, or vegetable oil
3 T. horseradish, freshly grated

Put egg yolk, mustard, vinegar, salt and pepper in a mixing bowl. Beat briskly with a wire whisk and gradually add oil until all is added. Stir in horseradish. Makes about one cup.

Sour Cream and Horseradish

Serve with smoked fish (sliced sturgeon, brook trout, etc.).

1 cup sour cream
3 T. horseradish, preferably freshly grated

Combine one cup of sour cream with 3 T. horseradish. Blend well. Makes about 1 cup.

Lemon-Butter Sauce
13 T. chilled unsalted butter cut into ½″ cubes
2 shallots, minced
Grated zest of 1 lemon
1 ½ T. fresh lemon juice
1 cup white wine
Salt to taste

In a saucepan over medium-low heat, melt 1 T. butter. Add shallots and zest; sauté, stirring, 4-5 minutes. Add juice and wine, reduce heat to low, and simmer until reduced to ⅓ cup, 20-25 minutes. Add butter, a few cubes at a time; whisk until blended before adding more. Strain sauce through a fine-mesh sieve. Season with salt. Makes about 1 cup.

Creole Sauce
½ cup (1 stick) butter
1 ½ cups chopped green bell pepper
1 ½ cups chopped onion
1 T. garlic, finely chopped
¼ cup tomato paste
2 T. paprika
1 ½ tsp. Italian seasoning
1 ½ cups chicken stock or water (optional)
1 cup tomato juice
1 cup peeled and chopped tomatoes
1 ½ tsp. Worcestershire sauce
1 ½ tsp. salt
Pinch of black pepper, cayenne, and white pepper
1 ½ T. cornstarch
2 T. water
¼ cup chopped fresh parsley

Melt butter in a large saucepan and cook the bell pepper, onion, celery and garlic until tender, 5-8 minutes. Sir in tomato paste, paprika, and Italian seasoning and cook an additional 3 minutes. Add 1 ½ cups chicken stock or water, tomato juice, tomatoes, Worcestershire sauce, salt, black cayenne, and white pepper. Bring mixture to a boil, then reduce heat and simmer for 8-10 minutes, stirring frequently.

In a small bowl, blend cornstarch with 4 T. water until smooth. Gradually add cornstarch to the mixture, stirring constantly, until sauce thickens. Sprinkle with parsley and serve.

Pesto
3 cups washed and dried fresh basil or 1 cup dried basil
1 cup washed and dried fresh spinach
3 cloves garlic
2 T. olive oil
⅓ cup pine nuts
½ cup butter
½ cup freshly grated Parmesan cheese
Freshly ground pepper
Salt

Finely chop basil and spinach in food processor. Add remaining ingredients and blend until smooth. Freeze in small packages (¼ cup). Thaw and use as desired.

Some serving suggestions: Put a dollop on any cream soup or tomato soup. Spread some on a steak or stir it into plain white rice. Mix with mayonnaise to make a dip for vegetables or a spread for hamburgers, adult style. Delicious spread on pita bread and briefly broiled or use on pasta.

Sweet-Sour Sauce
3 T. red wine vinegar
½ cup sliced scallion
Sauteed garlic
4 tsp. sugar
2 T. soy sauce
3 T. fresh orange juice
1 T. catsup
2 tsp. molasses
½ tsp. sesame oil
1 T. cornstarch in ¼ cup cold water

Stir ½ cup water, vinegar, garlic, sugar and simmer for 5 minutes. Stir in the rest of the ingredients and simmer for 2 minutes. Serve with cold chicken or pork.

20 Minute Spaghetti Sauce

1 lb. ground beef
1 small onion, chopped
1 clove garlic, minced
1 can (15 oz.) tomato sauce
½ cup red wine or water
1 T. Worcestershire Sauce
1 T. grated Parmesan sauce
½ tsp. salt
1 tsp. oregano
½ tsp. basil
½ tsp. sugar
Dash of pepper
4 oz. spaghetti, cooked and drained

In a large skillet, brown ground beef. Drain. Add onion and garlic. Cook until soft, about three minutes. Add tomato sauce, wine, Worcestershire sauce, Parmesan sauce, salt, oregano, basil, sugar, and pepper. Bring to a boil. Simmer over medium heat 20 minutes, stirring occasionally. Serve over cooked spaghetti. Makes 4 servings.

Balsamic Vinaigrette

1 tsp. fresh minced thyme
1 T. fresh minced Italian parsley
1 T. drained and minced capers
1 clove garlic finely minced
½ tsp. salt
Freshly ground pepper
5 T. good olive oil
1 ½ T. balsamic vinegar

Mix all ingredients except vinegar with a fork in a small bowl. Just before serving, whisk vinegar into mixture until slightly thickened. Pour over fresh salad greens.

Mediterranean Onion Relish

Serve as a relish with hamburgers or other charcoal-grilled meats and poultry; or as a tasty vegetable side dish, warm or cold.

2 T. olive or vegetable oil
1 ½ lbs. Spanish onions, cut in slivers
1 T. light brown sugar
1 can (16 oz.) whole tomatoes
¼ cup dry white wine or ¼ cup chicken broth

Combine all ingredients and simmer until well blended.

Bread & Butter Pickles

4 qts. sliced pickles
6 large sliced onions
6 T. salt

Soak in salted ice water for 2 hours or overnight.

1 qt. vinegar
4 cups sugar
1 T. celery seed
2 T/ mustard seed
½ tsp. tumeric powder

Boil syrup. Add pickles and onions and cook 4 minutes, stirring constantly. Pickles may be canned and then sealed.

Lindsey's Pie Crust

4 cups flour; 2 cups shortening. Mix until crumbs. In a cup measure, place 1 egg stirred and 1 tablespoon vinegar. Fill cup with milk. Stir well. Combine liquid ingredients with dry. Mix, cover and refrigerate. Makes 3 double crusts.

Perfect Nut Crust

10 oz. finely chopped walnuts or almonds
½ lb. (2 sticks) unsalted butter, softened
⅓ cup sugar
3 cups flour
1 egg, beaten
1 tsp. vanilla or almond extract

Preheat oven to 350º. Mix together all the ingredients until well blended, using an electric mixer or wooden spoon. Divide the mixture in half and press into 9-inch buttered spring-form tart pans; or press into twelve 3-inch tartlet pans. Chill for 30 minutes before baking for 15 to 20 minutes or until golden brown.

Cheesecake Brulée

16 oz. cream cheese
½ cup plus 4 T. sugar
2 T. sour cream
2 eggs
1 T. vanilla
1 cup graham cracker crumbs
4 T. (½ stick) unsalted butter, melted and cooled
2 T. brown sugar
¼ cup heavy cream

Preheat oven to 325º. Have a pot of boiling water ready. In bowl of an electric mixer, combine cream cheese, ½ cup sugar and sour cream; beat on medium speed until smooth. Add eggs, heavy cream and vanilla, beat until smooth.

In a bowl, combine graham cracker crumbs, butter and brown sugar; stir until blended and divide mixture among 4 mini-spring pans. With fingers, pat mixture evenly onto bottoms and divide cream cheese mixture among pans.

Line outside of pans with heavy-duty aluminum foil, shiny-side out; arrange them in a baking pan. Add boiling water to fill baking pan halfway up sides of spring-form pans. Bake until filling is set, 35-40 minutes. Refrigerate at least 3 hours.

Just before serving, unmold cheesecakes and sprinkle 1 T. sugar over each surface. With a kitchen torch, move flame continuously in small circles around surface until sugar melts, bubbles and lightly browns. Makes 4 mini-cheesecakes.

Lacy Dessert Baskets

¾ cup quick-cooking rolled oats
½ cup sugar
⅓ cup flour
¼ tsp. baking powder
6 T. butter or margarine, melted
2 T. milk
2 T. light corn syrup
Ice cream, slightly softened, or chilled
Whipped cream or topping
Frozen or fresh fruit

Blend all ingredients except ice cream and fruits in mixing bowl. Drop using level measuring tablespoon onto well-greased cookie sheets leaving plenty of space between (4 to a sheet). With back of a spoon, spread each to form a 3-inch cookie. Bake in preheated oven 375º for 6 minutes or until caramel-colored. Cool only ½ minute.

Working quickly, remove each cookie with a long, flexible spatula and place on an inverted 6 ounce custard cup; mold with hands to form basket. (If cookies harden before they are shaped, return to oven for 1 minute). Cool baskets before removing from cups. Just before serving, fill baskets with ice cream and garnish with fruit. Makes 18.

Marie-Chantal and Paul, 2006

shells completely before filling with Ricotta Filling. Use pastry tube to fill. Sift powdered sugar over shell. Garnish at ends with chopped chocolate and nuts. Makes 25

RICOTTA FILLING:
2 cups ricotta cheese (well drained)
1 cup whipped heavy cream
3 T. sugar
1 ½ tsp. vanilla extract

Put ricotta in a bowl; fold in whipped cream, adding sugar as you fold. Add vanilla. Refrigerate.

Cannoli

1 ¾ cups unsifted, regular all-purpose flour
½ tsp. salt
2 T. granulated sugar
¼ tsp. cinnamon
1 egg, slightly beaten
2 T. firm butter, cut in small pieces
Shortening or salad oil for deep frying
Ricotta filling ingredients
Powdered sugar
Chopped sweet chocolate & nuts for garnish
About ¼ cup dry Sauterne or any White
** wine**

Sift flour with salt, granulated sugar, and cinnamon. Make a well in the center; in it place egg and butter. Stir with a fork, working from center out, to moisten flour mixture. Add wine, 1 T. at a time, until dough begins to cling together. Use your hands to form dough into a ball. Cover and let stand for 15 minutes.

Roll dough out on floured board about $\frac{1}{16}$ inch thick. Cut into 3 ½-inch circles. With rolling pin, roll circles into ovals. Wrap around Cannoli forms; seal edge with egg white. Turn out ends of dough to flare slightly. Fry 2-3 at a time in deep hot fat (350º) for about one minute or until lightly golden.

Remove with tongs to paper towels to drain; let cool about 5 seconds; then slip out Cannoli form, holding shell carefully. Cool

Orleans Apple Torte
PASTRY:
$\frac{1}{3}$ cup sugar
$\frac{1}{3}$ cup butter
1 T. shortening
¼ tsp. vanilla
$\frac{1}{8}$ tsp. salt
1 cup flour

Cream together sugar, butter, and shortening. Add vanilla, salt, and flour. Blend well. Pat into the bottom and ½ inch up the sides of a lightly greased 9-inch spring-form pan.

TORTE:
4-5 Winesap apples
8 oz. cream cheese, softened
¼ cup sugar
1 egg
½ tsp. grated lemon peel
$\frac{1}{8}$ tsp. salt
¼ tsp. vanilla
Cinnamon and sugar
¼ cup sliced almonds

Pare, core and slice apples to measure 4 cups. Place apples in a shallow pan. Cover with foil and bake in a preheated 400º oven for 15 minutes while preparing filling. Beat cream cheese and sugar together. Add egg, lemon peel, salt, and vanilla. Beat until

smooth. Pour into prepared pastry crust. Top with partially cooked apple slices. Sprinkle with cinnamon, sugar and almonds. Bake at 400º for 40 minutes until apples are lightly browned. Cool well before cutting.

Mountain High Key Lime Pie

4 eggs, separated
1 can sweetened condensed milk
½ cup Key lime or Persian lime juice, strained
1 ½ tsp. grated Key lime or Persian lime peel
1 (9-inch) baked graham cracker crust, cooled
Whipped topping or sweetened whipped cream for topping

Preheat oven to 300º. Beat yolks of 4 eggs and the white of 1 egg until thick and lemon-colored. Add condensed milk and continue to beat well. Add juice and grated lime peel. Beat until thick. Beat the 3 remaining egg whites until stiff and fold into egg yolk mixture.

Pour into pie shell and bake for 15 minutes. (Any extra filling can be baked in a glass custard cup along with the pie.) Cool. Refrigerate for several hours before serving. Top with whipped topping or sweetened whipped cream.

Marie-Chantal's Birthday Keyboard Cake

24 oz. vanilla-flavored almond bark or Ghirardelli's white chocolate chips
1 pkg. (8 ½ oz.) cream-filled sugar wafer cookies
1 pkg. Keebler Fudge Sticks

Melt vanilla-flavored almond bark or chips following package instructions. Dip each wafer in melted bark or chips. Place each wafer, according to picture, creating the piano. Complete with fudge sticks while white chocolate is still warm. Happy Birthday!–*MaMa*

Chateau Chantal, 1993-2000

1993-2006

Changes of Color

In the heart
Of the forest
Changes of color
Are pulsing through,
Oranges and golds
And flaming reds
Burning.
Delicate aspens
Shimmer in satin
And velvet brown oaks
Soft whispers evoke.
I took small
Notice of you
In the green
Of your prime
Trickling away
With the passing
Of time.
And now your spirit
Shouts to me
From golden tresses
And rubied crowns,
Accept the changes
I've planned for you
The end is a beginning
A journey anew.

Tree limbs crack,
Their oaken bones
Grown stiff.
Softly, I tread
On sacred ground.
—EARLINE MCMILLIN

Marie-Chantal and Paul Dalese, October 14, 2006.

Don Quixote

Back to work. We have a three-room inn, which was such a delight to decorate. I not only prepared the breakfasts but also cooked up much fun and laughter. Three rooms meant six guests. I could handle that. It was great fun and I was confident...making many new friends. To this day many return every year.

In the meantime, my sweetest child attended Traverse City Public Schools. Marie-Chantal graduated in 1996 and moved to Chicago, Illinois. There she studied and graduated from De Paul University in 2000. A year at Adelaide University (Australia) in a Wine Management Program secured her education. Blessings abound! She met Paul Dalese in Australia. They were married on October 14, 2006.

The wedding day was truly beautiful and the happiest day in our lives. It began with Mass at St. Joseph's Church in Mapleton. Bishop Patrick Cooney (Bob's classmate) officiated at the ceremony along with Rev. Jim Meyer and Rev. Bob Singlelyn (also classmates). I chose to be in charge of the liturgy...beautiful music *"Panis Angelicus,"* and Gounod-Bach's *"Ave Maria"* as Chantal and I offered flowers to the Blessed Mother.

The reception, of course, was at Chateau Chantal. The weather was dark and dreary the entire day. As dinner was ending a glorious, flashing sunset descended upon us with beautiful autumn colors as a background. This sunset and the pictures taken were truly memorable. The goodness of God's love was clearly evident.

In 2003 we added seven new rooms to complete Bob's dream of a twelve-room inn. Twenty four people for breakfast? I don't think so. I still love to cook and manage two days a week with a bit of socializing on other days.

I satisfy my need to create by working with fabric. I have a small space in the tasting room called "Vineyard Couture". There you will find table runners, aprons, ironing board covers, place mats, shawls and scarves. All are welcome.

"Behold I stand at the door and knock, If anyone hears my voice and opens the door, I will enter his house and dine with him and he with me."–
REVELATIONS 21:3

The Recipes

Here it is –finally – my breakfast recipes, a ten-year collection. Since I also prepared the Wine Seminar Brunches for a time, I have included some of these creations.

1980-1993

RECIPES

BREAKFAST MAIN DISHES
Cheese Soufflé Roll w/Spinach Filling
Breakfast Pizza
Angel Puffs
Eggs Mornay with Fresh Tomato Sauce
Eggs Florentine with Asiago Cheese
Crustless Vegetable Quiche
Ham and Cheese Frittata
Eggs Benedict and Creamy Hollandaise Sauce
Geraldine's Basic Crepes
Pannakuku
Eggs-Artichoke Sausage Casserole
Cherry Cheese Strata
Creamed Eggs
Poached Eggs Chardonnay
Shrimp and Scrambled Eggs
Spinach Stuffed Portabello Mushrooms
Tomatoes Rockefeller

MUFFINS & QUICK BREADS
Glorious Muffins
Artichoke Bread
Apricot and Almond Muffins
Blueberry Muffins
Cranberry-Walnut Streusel Muffins
Cinnamon Swirl Bread
Raisin Pumpkin Bread

WAFFLES & TOAST
Crispy Waffles
Pumpkin Waffles
Peach French Toast
Very Cherry Stuffed French Toast
Raisin Cinnamon Toast

COOKIES
Oatmeal Cookies
Cherry Garcia Cookies
Belgian Molasses Cookies
Coconut Macaroon Cookies
Coconut Oat Cookies

PASTRIES
Cousin Lucille's Banquette
Cream Puffs
Easy Pecan Rolls
Double Cranberry Biscotti
Popovers
Luscious Apricot Bars
Canadian Sugar Pie
Polish Country Cheesecake
Select Harvest Gewurztraminer Cake
Pecan Tarts
Fresh Fruit Tarts
Almond Cakes

1980-1993

RECIPES

SOUP, SALADS, APPETIZERS
Bay Pointe Chowder Soup
Shrimp, Zucchini and Red Bell Pepper
  Bisque
Oyster and Brie Champagne Soup
Warm Goat Cheese Salad
Cheese and Wine Spread

SIDE DISHES
Roasted Root Vegetables with Apple Juice
  and Wine
Sugared Bacon
Smoked Whitefish Paté
Spinach Stuffed Onion Rings
Smoked Trout Cheesecake

CANDY
Divinity
Caramels
Chocolate Caramels
Vanilla Caramels
Icewine Truffles
Cherry Brandy Truffles
Chocolate Marquise
Pecan Roll
Butter Crunch
Opera Fudge
Crunchy Nutty Popcorn
Peanut Butter Balls

Cheese Soufflé Roll with Spinach Filling

7 eggs, separated
Butter or margarine
6 T. unsifted all-purpose flour
Dash cayenne pepper
¾ tsp. salt
1 ¼ cups milk
Parmesan cheese, grated
½ cup coarsely grated sharp Cheddar
  cheese
¼ tsp. cream of tartar

SPINACH FILLING:
2 packages (10 oz. size) frozen chopped
  spinach
2 T. butter or margarine
¼ cup finely chopped onion
¼ tsp. salt
¼ cup grated sharp Cheddar
½ cup sour cream
¼ lb. Cheddar cheese, sliced

Place whites and yolks in separate bowls. Let whites warm to room temperature, 1 hour. Grease bottom of a 15-by-10 ½-by-1-inch jelly roll pan. Line bottom with waxed paper; grease with butter. Heat oven to 350º. Melt ⅓ cup butter in saucepan.

Remove from heat. With wire whisk stir in flour, cayenne pepper, and ½ tsp. salt until smooth. Gradually stir in milk. Bring to boil, stirring. Reduce heat; simmer, stirring until thick and leaves bottom of pan. Beat in ½ cup Parmesan and ½ cup Cheddar.

With whisk beat yolks; beat in cheese mixture. With mixer at high speed, beat whites with ¼ tsp. salt and cream of tartar until stiff peaks form when beater is slowly raised. With under and over motion, fold one-third whites into the cheese mixture.

Carefully fold in remaining whites to combine. Turn into pan. Bake 15 minutes, or until surface is puffed and firm when pressed with fingertip. Meanwhile, make filling. Cook spinach as package label directs. Turn into sieve; press to remove water.

In hot butter on medium skillet, sauté onion until golden. Add spinach, salt, ¼ cup Cheddar and sour cream; mix well. With metal spatula loosen edges of soufflé. Invert on waxed paper sprinkled lightly with Parmesan. Peel off waxed paper.

Spread surface evenly with filling. Roll up from long side. Place, seam side down, on greased cookie sheet. Arrange cheese slices over top. Broil about 4 inches from heat just until cheese melts. Use large spatula to remove to serving dish or board. Serves 8.

Breakfast Pizza

1 lb. bulk pork sausage, crumbled
1 pkg. (8 oz.) refrigerated crescent rolls
1 cup frozen (loose-pack) hash brown
  potatoes, thawed
1 cup (4 oz.) shredded sharp Cheddar
  cheese or Mozzarella
½ green pepper, chopped
5 eggs
¼ cup milk
Salt and pepper
Parmesan cheese

In a skillet cook sausage until browned; drain and set aside. If using green peppers and onions, sauté with sausage. While sausage browns, beat together eggs, milk, salt and pepper (to taste) in mixing bowl.

Separate dough into 8 triangles and arrange in a pie pan with points toward center. Press over bottom and up sides to form crust (seal all perforations completely). Spoon sausage over crust. Sprinkle potatoes over sausage. Top with Cheddar cheese. Pour egg mix over fillings. Sprinkle Parmesan cheese over all and bake at 375º for 25-30 minutes. Yields 6-8 servings.

Angel Puffs

½ lb. shredded Cheddar cheese
1 tsp. baking powder
½ tsp. salt
12 eggs
½ lb. shredded Monterey Jack cheese
½ cup flour
1 pint cottage cheese

Preheat oven to 350º. Beat the eggs until light and fluffy. Add remaining ingredients and stir gently until well blended. Pour into a greased 9x13-inch baking dish. Bake for 30 minutes.

Variations: add ½ lb. cooked bacon, chopped Canadian bacon, chopped ham or chopped fresh broccoli.

Eggs Mornay with Fresh Tomato Sauce

FRESH TOMATO SAUCE:
3 medium sized ripe tomatoes
1 cup sliced mushrooms
2 T. olive oil
1 clove garlic, crushed
½ tsp. dried or fresh basil leaves
4 large eggs
1 cup chopped onions
2 slices natural Swiss cheese, halved lengthwise
5 slices toast, white or whole wheat
½ tsp. salt

Make fresh tomato sauce: Cut tomatoes into thin wedges. Cut off and discard cores. Put oil in a large skillet and heat over moderately high heat until oil is hot. Add garlic and basil; cook for 1 minute stirring occasionally.

Add fresh tomato wedges, mushrooms, onions, and salt to garlic and basil mixture in skillet. Cook several minutes tossing frequently with a wooden spoon until tomatoes are just heated through. Remove skillet from heat, cover and set aside to keep warm.

Prepare soft cooked eggs: Put eggs in a medium-sized saucepan and add cold water to measure 1-inch above eggs. Put pan over high heat and bring water to a boil. Remove pan from heat; cover and let stand 4 minutes. Cool eggs under running water to stop cooking.

When eggs are cool enough to handle, gently crack shells. Using fingers, gently remove and discard shells being careful not to break whites of the eggs. Wrap each egg in ½ slice of Swiss cheese. Set aside.

Divide tomato sauce evenly in shallow au-gratin dishes (each about 6 inches in diameter). Top sauce with a cheese wrapped egg. Place under hot broiler about 4 inches from heat source and broil 3-5 minutes or until cheese is melted and turns golden brown. Serve with buttered toast.

Eggs Florentine with Asiago Cheese

6 eggs, perfectly poached
3 English muffins
¼ cup butter
2 bunches fresh spinach
½ tsp. nutmeg
Salt and pepper to taste

ASIAGO CHEESE SAUCE:
2 scallions, finely chopped (white parts only)
½ cup white wine
4 cloves garlic, finely minced
1 cup shredded Asiago cheese
1 cup heavy cream

In a saucepan, combine garlic, scallions, and wine. Reduce sauce over medium high heat until wine is almost gone. Add cream and reduce again until mixture thickens noticeably. Add Asiago cheese and combine well. Keep sauce in a warm place until needed.

Slice and toast muffins and spread with butter. Add salt and pepper to spinach and sprinkle with approximately ¼ tsp. nutmeg. Place spinach atop buttered muffins. Lay poached eggs on top of spinach. Cover with cream sauce. Sprinkle with salt, pepper and nutmeg before serving.

Crustless Vegetable Quiche

1 cup chopped onions
1 cup chopped mushrooms
2 cups fresh spinach or zucchini
1 T. unsalted butter
1 cup cubed Havarti or sharp Cheddar
    Fontina
1 cup crumbled Feta cheese
½ cup Parmesan cheese
12-15 eggs
½ cup flour
½ cup half and half
6-8 drops of hot sauce
½ tsp. pepper
½ tsp. salt
½ tsp. thyme
½ tsp. salt

Sauté the first 4 ingredients until lightly browned. Drain well and place in greased baking dish (12x8-inch). Sprinkle the next 3 cheeses over the vegetables.

Process the eggs in a mixer at high speed; add the next seven ingredients and continue until blended. Pour over prepared vegetables and cheese. Sprinkle paprika, parsley, pepper; and add any other topping (tomatoes, olives, etc.). Bake at 350º for 40-45 minutes. Quiche should be puffed and golden brown.

Ham and Cheese Frittata

2 T. butter or margarine
½ cup sliced fresh mushrooms
½ cup chopped sweet red or green pepper
¼ cup sliced onions
6 eggs
1 tsp. water
½ cup diced cooked ham
1 cup (4 oz.) shredded Cheddar cheese

In an ovenproof skillet, melt butter over medium heat. Sauté mushrooms, peppers and onions until tender. Sprinkle with ham. Beat eggs until foamy. Pour over vegetables. Cook over medium heat for 5 minutes. Bake uncovered at 325º for 15 minutes or until a knife inserted near the center comes out clean.—*Paula Wasek*

Eggs Benedict and Creamy Hollandaise Sauce

6 thin slices of cooked ham
1 tsp. butter
3 split English Muffins
6 eggs, poached

CREAMY HOLLANDAISE SAUCE:
1 egg yolk
1 whole egg
1 pkg. (8 oz.) cream cheese, softened
Juice of 1 fresh lemon

In a small saucepan blend egg yolk and 1 whole egg into cream cheese beating vigorously. Blend in lemon juice. Cook over low heat stirring with a whisk until sauce thickens.

Toast and butter muffins. Fry ham in butter until slightly browned. Place 1 ham slice on cut side of muffin. Top with poached egg. Spoon warm sauce over eggs. Sprinkle with Parmesan cheese; pepper.

NOTE: Hollandaise sauce can also be used with ham-asparagus roll-ups with boiled sliced eggs.

Geraldine's Basic Crepes

1 ½ cups flour
1 to 3 T. sugar
½ tsp. baking powder
2 cups milk
2 eggs
1 to 2 tsp. vanilla
½ tsp. salt
3 T. butter or margarine

Combine eggs and sugar; whip for 10 minutes on third speed. On first speed, add milk and mix in. Add flour and mix until smooth. Add remaining ingredients; make a smooth batter. Add a small amount of batter to a preheated buttered crepe pan, swirling pan to coat bottom with batter. Cook over medium heat; when set, turn over and finish on the other side. Fill as desired. Makes 12 crepes.

Pannakuku

8 eggs
½ cup sugar
1 ¼ cup flour
Dash of nutmeg
½ tsp. salt
4 cups milk
¾ cups butter divided, melted

In a large bowl mix eggs, sugar, flour, salt, milk and ½ cup butter. Set aside. Heat remaining ¼ cup butter in a 9x13-inch pan. While oven heats to 400°, pour batter into prepared pan. Sprinkle with sugar and nutmeg. Bake for 30 minutes.

Remove from oven and cool for several minutes before cutting into squares. Serve with strawberry jam.—*Paula Wasek*

Eggs-Artichoke Sausage Casserole

2 lbs. bulk sausage, regular seasoning
½ lb. mushrooms, sliced
1 bunch green onions, finely sliced
12 slices bread, buttered on both sides, cut into triangles
2 cups mild Cheddar cheese, finely shredded
1 cup softened cream cheese
2 cans artichoke hearts, drained, chopped fine
2 tsp. Worcestershire sauce
3 cups milk
1 tsp. salt
Dash of Tabasco
1 tsp. paprika
1 tsp. dry mustard
2 dashes nutmeg
6 eggs

Spray 9x13-inch baking dish. Cook, drain and crumble sausage. Sauté mushrooms and onions. Line dish with 6 slice of bread, sprinkle and layer as follows: ½ sausage, ½ cup cream cheese, ½ mushrooms/onions, ½ artichoke hearts. Layer with remaining bread. Repeat layering remaining sausage, cheese, mushroom/onions and artichoke hearts.

Mix eggs, milk, seasonings and pour over ingredients. Refrigerate overnight. Bake 1 hour at 350° or until eggs are set. Top with sliced tomatoes and Parmesan cheese.

Cherry Cheese Strata

16 slices French bread
4 oz. cream cheese, softened
½ cup Chateau Chantal Cherry Merlot Jam
1 cup frozen cherries
4 eggs, slightly beaten
2 cups half & half
⅔ cup sugar
1 ½ tsp. finely shredded orange peel
Vanilla yogurt
¼ cup sliced almonds
¼ cup turbino sugar

Preheat oven to 350°. Spray a 2 quart square baking dish with cooking spray. Spread cream cheese on slices of bread and fit them into the baking dish in a single layer. Spread Cherry Merlot Jam over top. Scatter frozen cherries on top. Top each bread slice with another bread slice. Tear remaining bread into bite size pieces and fill in around the slices.

In a medium bowl combine eggs, half & half, sugar, orange peel and vanilla. Pour over bread in baking dish. Sprinkle with turbino sugar and sliced almonds. Bake uncovered about 45 minutes or until a knife inserted in the center comes out clean. Let stand 15 minutes before serving. Serve with vanilla yogurt. Makes 6 servings. —*Christine Campbell*

Creamed Eggs

10 T. butter
½ cup flour
1 ½ cups milk
1 ½ cups half & half
1 tsp. salt
¼ tsp. pepper
Dash of tarragon, cayenne pepper
½ lb. fresh mushrooms
6-8 hard-boiled eggs
¼ cup sherry
8 crisp toast triangles
Paprika

Melt 8 T. butter in a double boiler, stir in flour. Add combined milk and half & half slowly allowing sauce to thicken (medium thick). Add seasonings.

Sauté mushrooms in 2 T. butter until tender. Add sherry; simmer one minute. Stir into white sauce along with chopped egg whites. Adjust seasonings and pour over toast. Crumble yolks of eggs and sprinkle over top. Add a shake of paprika. Yields 6-8 servings.

For creamed ham: Add 3 cups chopped ham, ¼ cup finely chopped green onions (sautéed), and a dash of Worcestershire sauce to white sauce. Leave out tarragon and yolks of eggs.

Poached Eggs Chardonnay

1 T. butter
¼ cup Chateau Chantal Chardonnay
2 eggs
Grated Parmesan cheese
2 English muffin halves or 2 pieces toast
1 tsp. all-purpose flour
2 T. sour cream
White pepper
Salt to taste
Dash of paprika

In a small omelet pan, melt butter and add the Chardonnay; slip in the eggs. Sprinkle grated Parmesan generously over each egg. Cook over low heat until the whites are firm (covering the pan speeds up the process). Lift out the eggs onto slices of buttered/toasted English muffins or toast. Add the flour, sour cream, white pepper and salt to the liquid in the pan. Stir until combined and reaches a slight boil. Divide among the eggs and sprinkle with paprika.

Shrimp and Crab Scrambled Eggs

1 (7.5 oz.) can king crab meat
1 (4.5 oz.) can shrimp
3 T. sherry
8 T. butter or margarine
2 T. flour
¾ cup milk or half & half
1 T. chives
1 tsp. seasoning salt
1 tsp. salt
⅛ tsp. pepper
Few drops Tabasco
12 eggs

Drain and flake crab. Drain shrimp and combine with crab and sherry; set aside. Melt 6 T. butter in saucepan and remove from heat. Stir in flour until smooth and slowly add milk or cream. Bring to a boil stirring consistently. Reduce heat, simmer 1 minute. Stir in chives and shrimp mixture. (This can be prepared the day before and refrigerated.)

When ready to serve, whisk eggs, salt, pepper and Tabasco. In large skillet melt 2 T. butter, pour in eggs (low heat) and cook until partially done. Add seafood mixture and cook to desired doneness. Sprinkle with chives.

Poached Eggs Chardonnay

Tomatoes Rockefeller

Spinach-Stuffed Portabello Mushrooms

8 medium Portabello mushrooms, with
  stems and gills removed
10 oz. jar of roasted red peppers
½ pkg. fresh spinach, washed
8 large eggs
2 T. fresh chives, snipped
2 tsp. butter
1 cup Feta cheese
½ cup freshly grated Parmesan or Asiago
  cheese
Salt & pepper to taste

Preheat oven to 350º. Roast mushrooms in oven for about 15 minutes. Remove red peppers and blot dry. Microwave spinach on high for about 2 minutes until wilted. Set aside. In a medium bowl, whisk eggs. Add dash of salt and pepper and snipped chives. In a medium skillet melt butter. Add egg mixture and scramble. Add ½ cup Feta cheese.

  Line each mushroom cap with a layer of spinach leaves, then add a layer of roasted red pepper. Divide scrambled eggs mixture evenly on top. Sprinkle with remaining Feta and Parmesan cheese. Return to oven to melt cheese, about 2 minutes. Garnish with fresh herbs and tomatoes. Serves 8.

Tomatoes Rockefeller

12 thick tomato slices
2 (10 oz.) pkgs. frozen chopped spinach,
  cooked and drained
1 cup soft bread crumbs
1 cup seasoned bread crumbs
1 cup finely chopped green onions
6 eggs, slightly beaten
½ cup butter, melted
½ cup grated Parmesan cheese
1 tsp. thyme
¾ tsp. salt
½ tsp. minced garlic

Place tomato slices in a lightly greased 9x13-inch baking dish. Set aside. Press excess water from spinach and combine with remaining ingredients. Mound mixture on tomato slices. Bake at 350º for 15 minutes. Cover, if not served immediately. Serves 12.

Glorious Muffins

2 cups flour
1 ¼ cup sugar
2 tsp. baking soda
2 tsp. cinnamon
1 ½ cups shredded carrots
1 ½ peeled, shredded apples
¾ cup coconut
½ cup snipped dates
½ cup pecans
3 beaten eggs
1 cup oil
½ tsp. vanilla

In mixing bowl, combine flour, sugar, baking soda, cinnamon and ½ tsp. salt. In another bowl, combine carrots, apples, coconut, dates, and pecans. Stir in beaten eggs, oil, and vanilla. Add to dry ingredients stirring until moistened. Bake in greased muffin tins at 375º for 18-20 minutes. Serve with whipped cream cheese. Makes 24 muffins.

Artichoke Bread

3 cups loosely packed grated sharp
  Cheddar cheese
2 (6 oz.) jars marinated artichoke hearts,
  drained, finely chopped
6 soda crackers, crushed
4 eggs
3 green onion, finely chopped
Dash of hot pepper sauce
Salt and freshly ground pepper

Preheat oven to 335º. Grease an 8-inch square baking dish. Combine all ingredients in a large bowl and mix thoroughly. Turn into dish. Bake until tester inserted in center comes out clean, about 1 hour. Cool slightly before serving. Makes 6 servings.

Apricot and Almond Muffins

1 ½ cups flour
¼ cup ground almonds
2 tsp. baking powder
½ tsp. salt
¼ cup sugar
2 large eggs, beaten
4 T. butter, melted
¾ cup milk
1 cup dried apricots, finely chopped
1 tsp. lemon juice
¼ cup sliced almonds

Preheat oven to 400º. Grease a 12-cup muffin pan. Sift flour, ground almonds, baking powder, salt and sugar into a large bowl. Make a well in center and add eggs, butter and milk; mix lightly. Stir in chopped apricots and lemon juice. Spoon into greased muffin cups. Sprinkle with sliced almonds. Place in pan in preheated oven. Reduce temperature to 375º. Bake 25 to 30 minutes until well risen and golden. Remove muffins from cups and cool slightly on a wire rack.

Blueberry Muffins

1 ¼ cups fresh blueberries
2 cups all-purpose flour
½ cup plus 1 T. granulated sugar
1 T. baking powder
¼ tsp. baking soda
½ tsp. salt
1 large egg
1 cup buttermilk or plain yogurt
1 tsp. vanilla extract
5 T. unsalted butter, melted

Position a rack in the center of the oven and preheat to 400º. Line 12 (2 ½-inch) muffin cups with paper liners or generously butter both cups and top surface of muffin pan around the cups. Rinse blueberries and dry them on paper towels.

In a large mixing bowl stir together flour, ½ cup sugar, baking powder, baking soda,

and salt. Make a well in the center.

In a medium sized bowl whisk the egg and then whisk in buttermilk, vanilla, and melted butter. Pour this mixture into the dry ingredients. Quickly stir just to partially blend; add blueberries. Carefully fold together just to moisten; the batter will be thick and lumpy. Spoon into muffin cups dividing equally. Sprinkle tops with remaining one tablespoon sugar. Bake 25 to 30 minutes. Carefully remove and cool on a rack (If paper liners were not used, loosen each muffin and tilt it in its cups to prevent the bottoms from becoming soggy). Cool for 10 minutes. Serve warm.

Cranberry Walnut Streusel Muffins

1 cup fresh cranberries
1 T. all-purpose flour
1 T. sugar
1 ¾ cups all-purpose flour
2 ¾ tsp. baking powder
½ tsp. salt
½ cup sugar
1 tsp. nutmeg
1 tsp. grated orange rind
1 large egg, lightly beaten
⅔ cup milk
⅓ cup vegetable oil
½ cup chopped walnuts
Streusel topping

Combine first 3 ingredients in a small bowl and set aside.

Combine 1 ¾ cups flour and next five ingredients in a bowl; make a well in the center. Combine egg, milk, and oil. Add to dry ingredients, stirring just until moistened. Fold cranberry mixture and walnuts into batter. Spoon into greased muffin pans filling two-thirds full. Sprinkle with streusel topping. Bake at 400º for 18 to 20 minutes. Cool in pans on a wire rack for 5 minutes. Remove from pans. Yields 14 muffins.

STREUSEL TOPPING:
⅓ cup firmly packed brown sugar
1 T. all-purpose flour
1 T. butter or margarine
¼ cup chopped walnuts

Combine sugar and flour in a small bowl. Cut in butter with a pastry blender until mixture is crumbly. Stir in walnuts. Yields 1 cup.

Cinnamon Swirl Bread

1 ½ cups sugar, divided
1 T. ground cinnamon
2 cups all-purpose flour
1 tsp. baking soda
½ tsp. salt
1 cup buttermilk
1 egg
¼ cup vegetable oil

GLAZE:
¼ cup confectioners sugar
1 ½ to 2 tsp. milk

Combine ½ cup sugar and cinnamon; set aside. Combine flour, baking soda, salt, and remaining sugar. Combine buttermilk, egg, and oil. Stir into dry ingredients until combined.

Grease bottom of a 9x5x3-inch loaf pan. Pour half of batter into pan. Sprinkle with half of cinnamon-sugar. Carefully spread with remaining batter and sprinkle with remaining cinnamon-sugar. Swirl knife through batter.

Bake at 350º for 45-50 minutes or until a toothpick inserted near the center comes out clean. Cool in pan 10 minutes before removing to a wire rack to cool completely. Combine glaze ingredients. Drizzle over bread.—*Paula Wasek*

Raisin Pumpkin Bread

Tastes best if made a day in advance.

1 cup sugar
1 cup canned pumpkin
2 eggs, unbeaten
½ cup brown sugar, firmly packed
½ cup oil
2 cups sifted all-purpose flour
1 T. baking soda
½ tsp. salt
½ tsp. cinnamon
½ tsp. nutmeg
¼ tsp. ginger
½ tsp. baking powder
1 cup raisins
1 cup nuts
1 cup water

In a large mixing bowl combine sugar, pumpkin, eggs, brown sugar, and oil; beat until well-blended. Sift together flour, baking soda, salt, cinnamon, nutmeg, ginger, and baking powder. Combine with the liquid mixture mixing well. Fold in raisins, nuts, and water; turn into a well-oiled loaf pan. Bake at 350º for 65 to 75 minutes. Cool in loaf pan 5 minutes then turn out to cool thoroughly. Serves 16.

Crispy Waffles

2 cups flour
1 tsp. soda
1 T. sugar
1 tsp. salt
2 eggs, separated
¼ cup vinegar
1 ¾ cups sweet milk
4 T. melted shortening

Sift dry ingredients. Beat egg yolks, vinegar, and milk together. Add dry ingredients and then melted shortening. Blend well. Fold in egg whites, stiffly beaten. Bake on hot waffle iron. Serve with warm maple syrup.

Pumpkin Waffles

Pumpkin Waffles

16 oz. can pumpkin
1 ½ sticks butter (not margarine)
3 cups flour
5 tsp. baking powder
½ tsp. baking soda
½ tsp. cinnamon
½ tsp. nutmeg
½ tsp. ginger
⅛ tsp. salt
⅛ tsp. freshly ground pepper
3 eggs
⅓ cup packed brown sugar
2 ½ cups milk

Melt 1 ½ sticks butter and allow to cool. In a large bowl mix flour, baking powder, baking soda, cinnamon, nutmeg, ginger, salt, pepper and blend well with a wire whip. Beat eggs with brown sugar. Blend with pumpkin and milk. Add cooled butter and blend well.

Add pumpkin mixture to flour mixture and stir until ingredients are moist. Do not over beat. Bake in waffle iron at medium-high temperature. Waffles take about 7 minutes each.

Keep warm in a 200° oven. Place on oven racks with door ajar. Serve warm with hot apple butter. Makes seven 8-inch waffles.

Peach French Toast

1 cup brown sugar
½ cup butter or margarine
2 T. water
1 (29 oz.) can sliced peaches
6 eggs
2 cups milk
2 T. vanilla
1 loaf bread (French, white, Texan toast)

Drain peaches and reserve excess syrup. In a saucepan, heat butter and sugar on medium-low heat until butter is melted. Add water and continue cooking until sauce becomes thick and foamy. Pour into a 9x12-inch dish and cool for 10 minutes. Place peaches on top of cooled sauce and cover with slices of bread placed close together.

Thoroughly blend eggs, milk, and vanilla. Pour mixture over bread. Cover pan and refrigerate overnight. Bake at 350° for 40 minutes. If toast browns too quickly, cover loosely with foil for the final 10-15 minutes. Serve with warmed reserved peach syrup (or other syrup of choice). Garnish with fresh fruits.—*Paula Wasek*

Very Cherry Stuffed French Toast

8 eggs
1 tsp. vanilla
½ tsp. ground cinnamon
¼ tsp. ground nutmeg
¼ tsp. salt
12 slices dry white bread
1 (8 oz.) pkg. cream cheese, softened
¼ cup evaporated milk
1 (21 oz.) can cherry pie filling
2 T. butter
Granulated or powdered sugar (optional)
Maple flavored syrup (optional)

In a large mixing bowl, beat together eggs, evaporated milk, vanilla, cinnamon, nutmeg, and salt. Set aside.

Spread each slice of bread with cream cheese. Top six of the slices with cherry pie filling spreading almost to the edges. Cover each with the remaining bread slices, cream cheese side down. Dip in egg mixture.

In a skillet or on a griddle, cook sandwiches in hot butter over medium heat for 2 to 3 minutes on each side or until golden brown. Cut filled French toast into halves or leave whole and sprinkle with sugar, if desired. Serve with hot maple syrup.—*Bettie S. Fekaris*

Raisin Cinnamon French Toast

1 loaf Pepperidge Farm Swirl Raisin Cinnamon, cubed
6 eggs
3 cups milk
2 T. vanilla
1 cup cooked, sliced apples

Arrange bread cubes in greased 3-quart shallow baking dish. Mix all ingredients except apples. Pour over bread. Refrigerate overnight.

Mix $\frac{1}{2}$ cup flour, 6 T. brown sugar, $\frac{1}{2}$ tsp. cinnamon, and $\frac{1}{4}$ cup butter. Layer apples and sprinkle mix on toast just before baking. Bake at 350º for 50 minutes. Serves 8.

Oatmeal Cookies

1 $\frac{1}{2}$ cups old-fashioned oats
1 cup all-purpose flour
1 $\frac{1}{2}$ tsp. baking soda
$\frac{1}{4}$ tsp. salt
12 T. (1 $\frac{1}{2}$ sticks) unsalted butter, softened
1 cup (6 oz.) raisins
$\frac{3}{4}$ cup packed dark brown sugar
1 large egg
1 $\frac{1}{2}$ tsp. vanilla extract
1 T. water
1 cup (4 oz.) coarsely chopped walnuts

Position two (2) racks so that they are evenly spaced in the oven and preheat oven to 350º.

In a medium-sized bowl combine oats, flour, baking soda, salt and stir together. In a large bowl using a hand-held mixer set at high speed, cream butter until fluffy about 1 minute. Add egg, vanilla, and 1 T. of water; beat until thick and light 1 to 2 minutes. Stir in dry ingredients, walnuts, and raisins to make a thick dough.

Using 3 T. of dough for each cookie, drop dough onto lightly greased cookie sheets patting to flatten slightly. Place only 6 cookies on each sheet and leave about 4 inches between them. Bake 14-16 minutes until lightly brown around the edges reversing the sheets half-way through the baking, if one sheet of cookies browns sooner than the other.

Let cookies cool 2-3 minutes on the sheet to firm up slightly. With a spatula transfer cookies to absorbent paper. Let stand 5 minutes. Then transfer to a rack and cool to room temperature. Using a cool baking sheet continue to make the rest of the cookies. Makes about 1 $\frac{1}{2}$ dozen large cookies.

Cherry Garcia Cookies

1 cup dried tart cherries
$\frac{1}{3}$ cup cherry liqueur

Line two baking sheets with parchment paper. Plump dried cherries by covering with boiling water, drain well and toss with cherry liqueur and let sit for a couple of hours or even better overnight. Drain well before adding to cookie mixture.

COOKIE MIXTURE:
$\frac{1}{2}$ cup unsalted butter (room temp)
$\frac{1}{2}$ tsp. baking soda
$\frac{1}{2}$ cup sugar
$\frac{1}{2}$ cup brown sugar
1 egg
1 $\frac{1}{2}$ tsp. vanilla
$\frac{1}{4}$ tsp. almond extract
$\frac{1}{4}$ tsp. salt
1 $\frac{1}{2}$ cups flour
$\frac{3}{4}$ cup white chocolate, coarsely chopped
$\frac{1}{2}$ cup semi-sweet chocolate, coarsely chopped
$\frac{1}{2}$ cup Macadamia nuts, coarsely chopped (optional)

Preheat oven to 350º. Cream butter with sugars, blend in egg, vanilla and almond extract. Fold in salt, baking soda and flour. Fold in cherries, chocolates and nuts. Batter should be soft. Drop generous spoonful on baking sheet.

Bake at 350º until lightly brown around edges 12-14 minutes.

Belgian Molasses Cookies

Cream together:
1 cup butter
1 cup shortening
1 cup sugar

Add:
1 cup molasses
Sift approximately 4 ½ cups flour
1 tsp. baking soda
1 tsp. nutmeg
½ tsp. cloves
½ tsp. ginger
1 tsp. cinnamon

Add flour to make a dough which can be worked into rolls for slicing. Let stand overnight in refrigerator and slice very thin to bake. Bake at 350º for 10 minutes.

Coconut Macaroon Cookies

2 large egg whites
Pinch of salt
1 ½ cups (about 6 oz.) packed shredded sweetened coconut
3 T. all-purpose flour
⅓ cup sugar
1 tsp. vanilla extract

Evenly space 2 racks in the oven and preheat to 325º. Butter 2 baking sheets.

In a large mixing bowl, with a hand-held electric mixer, beat egg whites and salt together until soft peaks begin to form. Gradually add sugar and beat until stiff glossy peaks form, 1 to 2 minutes. Beat in vanilla. Add half of the coconut and sprinkle with flour. Add remaining coconut and fold together carefully and thoroughly.

Using 2 T. of the mixture for each cookie, drop onto baking sheets leaving about 3 inches between them. Place 9 on each sheet. Bake 18 to 20 minutes until light golden brown. Cool for 5 minutes and then transfer with a spatula to a rack to cool. Makes 1 ½ dozen.

Coconut Oat Cookies

1 cup butter or margarine
2 cups packed brown sugar
1 tsp. baking powder
1 tsp. vanilla extract
2 eggs
2 cup all-purpose flour
2 cups old fashioned oats
1 tsp. baking soda
1 tsp. salt
2 cups flaked coconut
Pecans

In a mixing bowl cream butter, brown sugar and vanilla. Add eggs one at a time beating well after each addition. Combine flour, oats, baking powder, soda, salt and coconut. Add to creamed butter-brown sugar mixture.

Drop a large spoonful on cookie sheet, press a pecan or two and sprinkle with sugar. Bake for 12 minutes at 350º.

Cousin Lucille's Banquette

4 cups flour
1 lb. unsalted butter
¾ cup water
2 T. vinegar

FILLING:
Almond pastry filling (12.5 oz.)
2 eggs
1 cup sugar

Cube and chill butter. Using a pastry blender, cut butter into flour mixture until coarse and crumbly. Add water and vinegar to flour mixture. Chill several hours. Roll out in two batches (18 in. x length of cookie sheet). Cut 4 ½-inch strips – 8 in all. If making one banquette, roll the strip as thin as possible.

Combine almond paste, 2 eggs and 1 cup sugar. Fill and seal dough with egg white. Brush with egg white and sprinkle with sugar. Bake at 450º for 15 to 20 minutes. The remaining dough can be frozen or filled with apple pie or poppy seed filling.—*Mary Bazzett, Traverse City*

Cream Puffs

½ cup butter (1 stick)
1 cup flour
1 cup boiling water
¼ tsp. salt
4 eggs

FILLING:
1 (12 oz.) carton Cool Whip
1 (3 oz.) French Vanilla Instant pudding
1 ¾ cups milk

Melt butter and water in a saucepan. Bring to a boil. Add flour and salt all at once and stir vigorously. Cook, stirring constantly, until mixture forms a ball. Remove from heat and cool slightly. Add eggs one at a time beating vigorously after each addition until mixture is smooth. Drop from tablespoon 2 inches apart onto greased baking sheet. Bake in hot oven (450º) for 15 minutes; then in moderate oven (325º) for 25 minutes. Remove with spatula and cool on rack. When thoroughly cool, slice off top of each puff.

While puffs are baking, make filling. Combine pudding and milk. Refrigerate until firm. Add Cool Whip and mix well. Fill puffs with cream and cover with sliced tops. Sprinkle with powdered sugar.

Easy Pecan Rolls

1 can of Pillsbury Grand Biscuits
2 cups chopped pecans
Brown sugar
Cinnamon
½ cup melted butter

Roll out each biscuit into a 5-inch by 10-inch rectangle. Generously sprinkle brown sugar, cinnamon and pecans. Roll up beginning with short side; cut in half; dip in butter. Bake in muffin tin (use Pam) for 20 minutes at 375º. Makes 16 pecan rolls.

Double Cranberry Biscotti

2 cups flour
1 ½ tsp. Calumet Baking Powder
¼ tsp. salt
½ cup (1 stick) butter or margarine, softened
1 ½ cups Post Selects Cranberry Almond Crunch cereal
2 eggs
1 tsp. vanilla
½ cup dried cranberries, chopped
¾ cup sugar

Heat oven to 325º. Mix flour, baking powder, and salt in small bowl. Beat butter and sugar in large bowl with electric mixer on medium speed until light and fluffy. Beat in eggs and vanilla. Gradually add flour mixture beating well after each addition. Stir in cereal and dried cranberries.

Divide dough into 2 equal portions; place on greased cookie sheet. Shape each portion into log 14" long and 2" wide.

Bake 30 minutes or until lightly browned. Remove from cookie sheet. Place on cutting board; cool 10 minutes. Using serrated knife, cut each log into diagonal slices about ¾ inches thick. Place slices upright on cookie sheet about ½ inch apart. Bake 12 minutes or until slightly dry. Remove from cookie sheet. Cool on wire rack. Store in tightly covered container. Makes about 2 dozen.

Popovers

1 ¼ cups milk
1 ¼ cups flour
½ tsp. salt
3 jumbo or 4 large eggs

Preheat oven to 425º. Generously grease popover cups. Pour milk into a medium size bowl. Add flour and salt. Beat until well blended. (Do not over beat.) Add eggs one at a time, beating in each until completely blended. Fill cups ¾ full. Bake at 425º for 20 minutes. Reduce temperature to 325º and continue baking for 20 minutes or until golden brown. Serve with jam.

Luscious Apricot Bars

½ cup Gewurtztminer wine
1 cup California dried apricots
1 stick (½ cup) unsalted butter, softened
¼ cup granulated sugar
1 ⅓ cups all-purpose flour
1 cup packed light brown sugar
2 large eggs
1 cup chopped walnuts (2 ¼ oz.)
½ tsp. baking powder
½ tsp. vanilla
¼ tsp. salt
Confectioners sugar for dusting

Preheat oven to 350º. Simmer apricots in Gewurztraminer wine to cover in a small saucepan, covered, for 15 minutes. Drain, then cool to room temperature and finely chop.

Beat together butter, granulated sugar, and 1 cup flour with an electric mixer on medium speed until mixture resembles coarse crumbs. Press evenly over bottom of a greased 8-inch square metal baking pan (nonstick) and bake in middle of oven until golden, about 25 minutes.

Beat together, in same bowl, chopped apricots, brown sugar, eggs, walnuts, baking powder, vanilla, salt, and remaining ⅓ cup flour on medium speed until combined well. Pour topping over crust and bake in middle of oven until topping sets and becomes golden for about 25-30 minutes more. Cool in pan on a rack and cut into 12 bars. Dust with confectioners' sugar.

Canadian Sugar Pie

2 cups brown sugar
4 tsp. flour
2 tsp. milk
1 T. corn syrup
1 ½ tsp. softened butter
1 pastry crust
½ cup of cream

Mix brown sugar and flour. Add next 3 ingredients. Turn into pastry lined pan and pour ½ cup of cream Bake at 350º for 40-45 minutes.–*Jacquie Begin*

Polish Country Cheesecake

DOUGH:
1 ¾ cup all-purpose flour
½ cup confectioners sugar
¾ tsp. baking powder
¼ tsp. salt
¼ cup butter
3 egg yolks
3 T. dairy sour cream

FILLING:
4 eggs plus 1 egg white
¾ cup sugar
1 ½ lbs. Farmers ricotta or pot cheese
½ cup sour cream
2 T. grated orange peel
1 tsp. vanilla extract

To make dough: combine flour, sugar, baking powder and salt in a bowl. Using a pastry blender, cut butter into flour mixture until coarse and crumbly. Beat egg yolks into sour cream. Stir into flour mixture. Knead in bowl until dough is well mixed and holds its shape. Refrigerate dough until it is easy to roll out, at least 2 hours. Roll dough on a floured surface to fit a 13x9x2-inch pan. Line bottom of pan fitting dough so it comes about ⅔ on the way up the sides of the pan.

Filling: Beat eggs and egg white at high speed of electric mixer until thick. Gradually add sugar, beating at high speed until stiff, not dray, peaks form. Press cheese through a sieve. Fold into beaten egg mixture. Add remaining ingredients and mix gently but thoroughly.

Turn filling into dough-lined pan. Bake at 350º about 40 minutes or until set. Cool before cutting into squares.

Select Harvest Gewurztraminer Cake

18 oz. yellow cake mix
1 small package vanilla pudding, instant
½ cup water
1 cup Chateau Chantal Select Harvest
  Gewurztraminer
½ cup vegetable oil
4 eggs
½ cup pecans, chopped
¼ lb. butter
1 cup sugar
¼ cup water

Line bottom of greased 10-inch tube pan with chopped pecans. Blend boxed cake mix, pudding, ½ cup water, ½ cup Select Harvest Gewurztraminer, ½ cup vegetable oil, and 4 eggs with mixer and pour into pecan-lined tube pan. Bake at 325° for 50-60 minutes.

Mix and boil for 3 minutes the following: butter, sugar, and ¼ cup water. Remove from heat and then add remaining Select Harvest Gewurztraminer. Pour this mixture over hot cake and leave in pan until completely cool before turning out. Serves 16.

Pecan Tarts

½ cup unsalted butter
½ cup sugar
2 egg yolks
1 tsp. almond extract
2 cups flour, sifted

Mix above ingredients and press evenly into tiny tart shells or muffin cups. Bake in 400° oven 8 to 10 minutes.

½ cup margarine
⅓ cup dark corn syrup
1 cup confectioners sugar
1 cup chopped pecans

Bring to boil margarine, syrup, and sugar; stir in pecans. Spoon into shells and top with pecan halves. Bake in 350° oven 5 minutes. Makes 4 dozen.

Fresh Fruit Tarts

PASTRY:
½ cup confectioners' sugar
¼ tsp. salt
½ cup butter, cut into pieces and softened
2 egg yolks beaten
3 T. cold water
2 cups all-purpose flour

FILLING:
¾ cup vanilla milk chips
3 T. whipping cream
4 oz. cream cheese, softened
Assorted fresh fruits: bananas, blueberries,
  grapes, kiwis, mandarin oranges, or
  strawberries

GLAZE:
⅔ cup apple jelly
2 tsp. granulated sugar

For pastry, combine sugar and salt in a bowl. Cut in butter with a pastry blender or 2 knives until almost blended. Combine egg yolks and water in a small bowl; stir into butter mixture. Add flour, mixing just until blended. Divide dough in half and wrap in plastic wrap. Refrigerate at least 1 hour.

Preheat oven to 350°. Working with half of the dough at a time, press about 1 tablespoon of dough into each small tart pan. Prick bottoms and sides of shells with a fork. Place on baking sheets and bake 20 to 25 minutes or until lightly browned. Cool on wire rack.

For filling, melt vanilla chips with cream in a double boiler over medium heat, stirring until smooth. Remove from heat and beat in cream cheese. Spoon filling into cooled pastry shells.

Decorate with assorted fruits. For glaze, melt jelly and sugar in a small saucepan over low heat; cool slightly. Brush gently over fruits. Chill several hours before serving. Yield: about 18 tarts.

Fresh Fruit Tarts

Almond Cakes

¾ cup sliced almonds
½ cup butter
1 ½ cups granulated sugar
3 egg yolks
1 ½ cups all–purpose flour
½ tsp. baking soda
½ cup sour cream
1 tsp. almond extract
3 egg whites, room temperature

TOPPING:
1 cup Sanders Caramel Sauce flavored with
  ¼ cup Amaretto or Almond Extract
2 T. whipping cream

Preheat oven to 325º. Grease and flour a 6-mold Bundt pan. Sprinkle almonds in bottoms of each mold. In a large bowl, cream butter and 1 ¼ cups sugar. Add egg yolks, one at a time, beating well after each addition. In a separate bowl, combine flour and baking soda. Add to creamed mixture alternately with sour cream, beginning and ending with flour mixture. Stir in almond extract.

In a medium bowl, beat egg whites until foamy. Add ¼ cup sugar, 1 tablespoon at a time, beating until stiff peaks form. Fold into cake batter. Pour into pans and bake 20 to 25 minutes, testing for doneness with a toothpick. Cool in pans 15 minutes.
While cakes are cooling in pans, combine sauce ingredients in a small saucepan. Boil 4 minutes, stirring constantly. Remove cakes from pans; place on a wire rack with waxed paper spread underneath. While cakes are still warm, use a fork or wooden skewer to poke holes in cakes. Spoon warm sauce over cakes. Allow cakes to sit at least 1 hour. Serve warm.

Bay Pointe Chowder Soups

2 t. butter
½ cup diced celery, onion, carrots
¼ cup diced tomatoes, seeds removed
⅓ lb. diced raw shrimp
⅓ lb. diced raw clams
⅓ lb. diced raw lobster
¼ cup fresh lemon juice
½ cup diced blanched redskin potatoes
1 ½ oz. cream sherry
1 pint rich homemade chicken stock
1 qt. heavy whipping cream
1 tsp. salt
1 tsp. white pepper
1 tsp. Paprika

ROUX:
8 oz. melted butter with ⅓ cup flour

Melt butter and combine celery, onions, and carrots. Sauté until onions are clarified. Add shrimp, clams, and lobster and continue to sauté until slightly cooked. Add tomatoes and cream sherry and cook for 3 minutes.

Add chicken stock, cream and seasonings. Simmer 20 minutes. Combine melted butter with flour into a smooth paste and cook over low heat for 5 minutes. Raise heat on simmering chowder and add roux, a third at a time, whisking briskly. Simmer for 2 to 3 minutes each time.

After roux is added, stir in redskins and simmer soup for 20 minutes. Season to taste and serve immediately. Serves 6-8.

Shrimp, Zucchini and Red Bell Pepper Bisque

1 lb. uncooked large shrimp
7 T. butter
¾ cup chopped onion
¾ cup chopped celery
3 cups cold water
2 cups bottled clam juice
1 cup Chateau Chantal Chardonnay
2 fresh parsley sprigs
¼ tsp dried thyme
¼ tsp. whole black peppercorns
⅓ cup flour
¼ cup Madeira
3 T. tomato paste
¾ cup half and half
1 medium zucchini cut into ¼ inch cubes
1 medium-size red bell pepper cut into
   ¼ inch cubes

Peel and devein shrimp; reserve shells. Coarsely chop shrimp. Place shrimp in small bowl, cover and refrigerate.

Melt 1 T. butter in heavy medium saucepan over medium heat. Add onion and celery. Cover and cook until tender, stirring occasionally, about 5 minutes. Add reserve shrimp shells, 3 cups cold water and next 5 ingredients. Bring liquid to boil. Reduce heat to low and simmer until liquid is reduced to 5 cups, about 30 minutes. Strain shrimp stock; discard solids.

Melt 4 T. butter in heavy large pot over medium heat. Add flour and whisk until mixture bubbles but does not brown, about 3 minutes. Whisk Madeira and tomato paste, then shrimp stock. Simmer until mixture thickens slightly, about 8 minutes. (May be prepared a day ahead. Cool slightly. Cover and refrigerate. Bring soup to simmer before continuing). Mix in half and half. Cook until soup is heated through (do not boil). Season soup to taste with salt and pepper.

Meanwhile, melt remaining 2 T. butter in heavy large skillet over medium-high heat. Add zucchini and red bell pepper. Sauté until vegetables are crisp-tender about 3 minutes.

Add reserved shrimp. Sauté just until shrimp is cooked through and vegetables are tender about 3 minutes longer. Season shrimp mixture with salt and pepper.

Spoon ⅓ cup shrimp mixture into center of each bowl. Ladle soup around shrimp mixture and serve. Serves 8.

Oyster and Brie Champagne Soup

½ lb. unsalted butter
½ cup flour
1 qt. oyster water or seafood stock
   or bottle clam juice
5 cups whipping cream
1 ½ lbs. brie cheese, rind removed, cut into
   small squares
2 cups dry champagne
3 dozen oysters
1 cup green scallion stems, finely minced
Salt to taste

In a 3-quart saucepan melt butter over low heat; add flour and cook 3 minutes, whisking constantly. Add stock and continue to cook and whisk until flour is absorbed, about 3 to 4 minutes. Bring to a boil; return to simmer for 10 minutes whisking occasionally.

Add cream, simmer 5 minutes, again whisking constantly. Add cheese, whisking until completely melted. Add oysters and green onions. Cover and let stand for 10 minutes. Taste for seasoning; stir, and serve.

Warm Goat Cheese Salad

8 oz. Goat cheese
8 slices French bread
³/₄ tsp. dried thyme
3 small heads Boston or Butter lettuce
5 T. extra Virgin Olive Oil
1 tsp. Dijon mustard
1 tsp. best quality red or white wine vinegar
Salt and freshly ground pepper to taste

MAKE GOAT CHEESE CROUTONS:
Preheat broiler. If goat cheese comes in a log shape, cut into 8 slices of equal thickness and place one on each slice of bread. Arrange on broiler pan. Using one T. of olive oil, drizzle over goat cheese and sprinkle with dried thyme.

Broil 3 to 5 minutes, watching carefully so the bread does not burn. Remove when goat cheese has softened and has started to become golden, but before it has melted and lost its shape.

MAKE VINAIGRETTE:
Mix vinegar and mustard thoroughly. Slowly whisk in remaining 4 T of olive oil. Season to taste with salt and pepper. Toss with greens and place on salad plates. Arrange two goat cheese croutons on each salad and serve.

Cheese and Wine Spread

Originally printed in the Traverse City Record Eagle, *November 5, 1990, 1B*

8 oz. Fontina cheese, cubed,
  at room temperature
3 oz. Herbed cream cheese,
  at room temperature
2 oz. Bleu cheese, crumbled,
  at room temperature
¼ cup Chateau Chantal Chardonnay
1 tsp. Dijon mustard
1 T. packed fresh parsley leaves
Assorted crackers
Red, green, or blue/black grapes

Combine all ingredients, except crackers and grapes, in blender or food processor. Blend until smooth and thoroughly combined. Serve with crackers and fresh grapes. Makes 1 ½ cups spread.

Roasted Root Vegetables with Apple Juice and Wine

3 cups apple juice
1 cup semisweet white wine (such as
  Gewurztrminer or Riesling)
3 T. butter
1 ¼ lbs. turnips
1 ¼ lbs. parsnips
1 ¼ lbs. carrots
1 ¼ lbs. red-skinned sweet potatoes (yams)
1 ¼ lbs. beets

Boil apple juice and wine in a heavy large saucepan until reduced to ¼ cup, about 30 minutes. Whisk in butter.

Preheat oven to 425º. Peel and cut vegetables into ½ inch pieces. Divide between 2 large roasting pans. Pour apple juice mixture over vegetables. Sprinkle with salt and pepper. Toss to coat. Roast until vegetables are tender and golden, stirring occasionally, about 40 minutes. Serves 8.

Sugared Bacon

Thick Cut Bacon
Brown sugar
Pepper

Heat oven to 400º. Twist and pull bacon placing it on a greased tray. Bake bacon until 90% of fat is extracted. Drain. Lower temperature to 300º. Generously sprinkle bacon with brown sugar and pepper. Complete the baking allowing sugar to crystallize.

**Roasted Root Vegetables
with Apple Juice and Wine**

Smoked Whitefish Paté

1 lb. smoked whitefish filet meat, cleaned
and deboned
1 ³/₄ lbs. cream cheese, softened
Worcestershire sauce to taste
Tabasco sauce to taste

Place cleaned smoked whitefish in electric mixing bowl and mix on slow speed for 1 minute. Stop mixer. Check inside bowl for any bones that may have been missed. Add cream cheese and mix for 2 minutes on medium speed. Scrape mixing bowl. Mix again for 1 minute.

Check that all smoked whitefish and cream cheese is mixed well. Season very lightly with Tabasco and Worcestershire sauces. May be served with crackers and jalapeno salsa. May also be served hot, baked in a casserole.

Spinach Stuffed Onion Rings

12 oz. beer, room temperature
1 ½ cups flour
½ tsp. salt
4 large white onions
Vegetable oil for frying
1 (10 oz.) pkg. frozen creamed spinach,
cooked

Mix beer, flour, and salt. Let sit for 1 hour. Slice onions 1 inch thick. Separate into rings (6 to 8 outer rings to an onion; discard centers). Heat oil in deep fat fryer to 375º. Dip rings in batter. Fry until golden brown, about 2-3 minutes. Drain on paper towel. Store at room temperature, covered, until final baking.

Place rings on an oiled baking sheet and fill with spinach. Bake at 350º for 15-20 minutes or until spinach bubbles. Cooking time: 40 minutes. Serves 12

Smoked Trout Cheesecake

CRUST:
2 cups roasted finely chopped pecans
2 T. butter

FILLING:
24 oz. cream cheese, cubed
6 eggs
1 pint sour cream
⅓ cup sifted flour
Juice of ½ lemon
Grated zest of ½ orange
1 ½ cups flaked smoked trout
1 cup chopped green onions
Grated zest of 1 lemon
Salt and pepper to taste
Grated zest of ½ lime
Tabasco sauce to taste

Mix 1 ½ cups of pecans with butter to line the bottom of a 10-inch springform pan. Butter sides of pan well. Preheat oven to 350º. Beat cubed cream cheese until soft and creamy. Blend in eggs one at a time until well blended. Add sour cream, flour, zests of lemon, lime, and orange, and lemon juice. Mix well. Stir smoked trout and green onions into cheese mixture and add salt, pepper, and Tabasco.

Pour cheese mixture into prepared pan and bake for 1 hour. Turn off heat and allow cheese cake to remain in the oven for another hour. Cool to room temperature. Sprinkle remaining nuts on top of the cake. Chill overnight. May be served with Sour and Sweet Red Onions, whole grain mustard, diced tomatoes.

Smoked Trout Cheesecake

Cherry Brandy Truffles
(RECIPE PG. 116) **and**
Luscious Apricot Bars
(RECIPE PG. 105)

Divinity

2 ½ cups of sugar
⅔ cup light corn syrup
½ cup water
¼ tsp. salt
2 egg whites, stiffly beaten
½ tsp. vanilla
¼ cup chopped red maraschino cherries
¼ cup chopped green maraschino cherries
1 cup chopped English walnuts

Combine sugar, corn syrup, water and salt in saucepan; heat, stirring, until sugar is dissolved. Boil, without stirring, until syrup reaches hard-ball stage. Remove from heat. Pour syrup gradually into egg whites, beating constantly with electric beater at medium speed. Beat until mixture holds shape when dropped from spoon. Stir in vanilla, cherries and walnuts.

Place in lightly greased 9-inch square pan. Cut in 1-inch squares. Divinity may be dropped from spoon onto waxed paper, if desired. Yield: 1 ¼ lbs.

Caramels

2 cups sugar
2 cups light corn syrup
⅛ tsp. salt
½ cup (1 stick) unsalted butter
2 cups Pet Evaporated milk
1 tsp. vanilla

In a 3-quart heavy saucepan, combine sugar, corn syrup, and salt. Cook over medium-high heat until mixture reaches firm-ball stage (244º) stirring occasionally. Add butter and gradual-ly add evaporated milk so that mixture does not stop boiling. Stirring constantly, cook rapidly to firm-ball stage again.

Remove from heat; add vanilla and pour mixture into a buttered 9x9-inch baking pan without scraping the sides of the saucepan. Cool thoroughly before cutting. Makes 81 caramels.

Chocolate Caramels

1 cup sugar
¾ cup light corn syrup
3 squares unsweetened chocolate
¼ tsp. salt
1 ½ cups heavy cream
1 tsp. vanilla

Combine sugar, corn syrup, chocolate, salt, and ½ cup cream. Cook over low-medium heat stirring constantly until sugar is dissolved and the mixture boils. Continue boiling and add another ½ cup cream. Boil to 230º stirring constantly.

Add remaining ½ cup cream and boil until a firm ball forms in cold water (237º). Pour into a slightly buttered pan (8x8-inches). DO NOT scrape the pot. Let stand until cold. Cut and wrap in wax paper. Makes 40 caramels. Do not refrigerate.

Vanilla Caramels

1 cup sugar
1 ¾ cups heavy cream
¼ cup light corn syrup
1 tsp. vanilla
½ tsp. salt

Combine sugar, corn syrup, chocolate, salt, and ½ cup cream. Cook over low-medium heat stirring constantly until sugar is dissolved and the mixture boils. Continue boiling and add another ½ cup cream. Boil to 230º stirring constantly.

Add remaining ½ cup cream and boil until a firm ball forms in cold water (237º). Pour into a slightly buttered pan (8x8-inches). DO NOT scrape the pot. Let stand until cold. Cut and wrap in wax paper. Makes 40 caramels. Do not refrigerate.

Icewine Truffles

⅓ cup whipping cream
2 T. butter, softened
½ lb. Callebaut chocolate
¼ cup cocoa powder
⅓ cup Chateau Chantal Icewine
1 tsp. powdered sugar

Bring cream to a boil and add to chocolate in a bowl. Blend, then stir in Icewine. Beat in butter when cool. Set aside until firm enough to handle. Then drop mixture by small spoonful into a shallow dish of cocoa powder sweetened to taste with powdered sugar.

Roll each truffle in cocoa rounding it between the palms of your hands. Dust hands with cocoa as necessary to keep truffles from sticking. If truffles are too hard to shape, wait until they soften. If too soft, chill until firm. Truffles look more authentic if a little irregular in shape.

Shake truffles gently in a dry strainer to remove excess cocoa, if necessary. Store in an airtight container in the refrigerator up to 10 days or in a freezer up to 3 months. Remove from refrigerator 30 minutes before serving to soften slightly. Serve in a candy dish or place each truffle in a fluted paper cup. Makes 3 dozen small truffles.

Cherry Brandy Truffles

1 lb. Callebaut milk chocolate
1 cup whipping cream
½ cup Chateau Chantal Cerise
4 T. unsalted butter
½ lb. Callebaut bittersweet chocolate for dipping

Break up chocolate in small pieces. Melt in double boiler over simmering water. Add butter and whipping cream and cerise. (Finely chopped nuts may be added.) Chill until firm enough to roll into 1-inch balls. Freeze.

Dip into melted bittersweet chocolate. Can be drizzled with white chocolate or decorated with nuts.

Chocolate Marquise

½ lb. butter
10 oz. chocolate
8 eggs, separated
¼ cup Cognac

Mix butter and chocolate. Refrigerate 15 minutes. Stir in egg yolks one at a time. Add cognac; beat egg whites to soft peaks and fold in. Freeze for 3 hours.

Pecan Roll

1 lb. sifted powdered sugar
1 jar marshmallow crème
1 lb. caramels
Pecans, chopped

Knead together powdered sugar and crème. Roll into 6 logs. Freeze. Melt 1 lb. caramels with a little milk or cream. Dip frozen log in caramel and roll in pecans. Do one at a time.

Butter Crunch

2 cups chopped almonds
2 cups butter (1 lb.)
2 cups sugar
⅔ cup brown sugar
4 T. water
1 tsp. Baking soda
1 cup semi-sweet chocolate chips

Butter a 12x18-inch baking pan with sides. Sprinkle in 1 cup almonds. Melt the butter; add sugar and water. Boil, stirring constantly until sugar is dissolved. Cook (do not stir) until 300º. Remove; stir in baking soda; pour over almonds. Cool 15 minutes. Sprinkle chocolate chips. Melt and spread. Add remaining almonds.

Opera Fudge

2 cups granulated sugar
½ cup milk
½ cup light cream
1 T. light corn syrup
½ tsp. salt
1 T. butter or margarine
1 tsp. vanilla
½ cup nuts

Butter sides of a heavy 2-quart saucepan. Combine sugar, milk, cream, corn syrup, and salt. Cook over medium heat stirring constantly until sugar dissolves and mixture comes to a boil. Cook to soft-ball stage (238º).

Immediately remove from heat and cool to lukewarm (110º) without stirring. Add butter and vanilla. Beat vigorously until mixture becomes very thick and loses its glaze. Quickly stir in chopped nuts and spread in a buttered 9x5x3-inch pan. Score in squares while warm. Cut when cool and firm.

Peanut Butter Balls

3 cups powdered sugar
3 T. cream
2 cups crunchy peanut butter
1 stick unsalted butter, softened
1 tsp. vanilla
1 lb. Callebaut or Hershey's chocolate

Combine first 5 ingredients. Form into balls. Refrigerate or freeze until firm. Dip balls in melted chocolate and place on wax paper. Cool until firm.

Crunchy Nutty Popcorn

2 qts. popped corn, no butter or salt added
1 ⅓ cups chopped pecans
⅔ cup chopped almonds
1 ⅓ cups sugar
1 cup butter
½ cup corn syrup
1 tsp. vanilla

Mix popped corn, pecans, and almonds together in a very large, slightly greased bowl. Set aside.

In a heavy 1 ½ quart saucepan combine sugar, butter, and corn syrup. Bring to a boil over medium heat stirring constantly about 15 minutes or until mixture turns a light caramel color. Remove from heat and stir in vanilla.

Pour immediately over corn/nut mixture working quickly to toss and coat corn and nuts. Quickly spread out to dry on a lightly greased cookie sheet. Speed is important. When dry and brittle, break into chunks and store in a tightly covered container. Makes about 2 pounds.

RECIPE INDEX

1932-1950
FAMILY DAYS

SOUPS & SALADS
Duck Soup *(Czarnina)* **10**
Dumplings **10**
Old Fashioned Tomato Bisque **10**
Dill Pickle Soup **10**
Cabbage Salad **11**

MAIN DISHES
Chop Suey **11**
Kielbasa **11**
Baked Ham *(Szynka)* **11**
Chili Con Carne **12**
Baked Oysters **12**
Cheese or Plum Dumplings *(Pierogi)* **12**

VEGETABLES & SIDE DISHES
Cornmeal Mush **13**
Potato Pancakes **13**
Egg Pancakes **13**
Cucumbers in Sour Cream **13**
Wax Beans in Sweet-Sour Sauce **14**
Dandelion Greens **14**

BREAD, PASTRY, DESSERTS
White Bread **14**
Plain Yellow Cake **14**
Mom's Apple Pie and Glaze **15**
Mom's Custard Pie **15**
Bread Pudding **15**
Mystery Cake of 1932 **16**
Vanilla Butter Frosting **16**
Johnny Cake **16**
Aunt Carolyn's Popcorn Balls **16**
Mom's Coconut Cream Pie **18**
Polish Bows *(Chrusciki)* **18**
Mom's Special Tomato Preserves **18**
Genevieve's Upside Down Cake **19**

1950-1972
CONVENT DAYS

SOUPS & SALADS
Beet Soup *(Barszcz)* **32**
Sauerkraut Soup *(Kapusta)* **32**
Uptown Convent Fruit Soup **32**

MEATS & VEGETABLES
Meatloaf **32**
Stuffed Cabbage Rolls *(Golabki)* **33**
Turkey Paprika with *Kluski* **33**
Easy Noodles *(Kluski)* **33**

BREAD, PASTRY, DESSERTS
Convent *Babka* **34**
Small *Babka* **34**
Kolacky **35**
Polish Donuts *(Paczki)* **35**
Poppy Seed Roll **35**

1972-1980
JUST NADINE, DETROIT AND MARRIAGE

APERITIF
Mock Champagne Punch **46**
Shrimp Cocktail with Brandy and Cream **46**

SOUPS
French Canadian Pea Soup **46**
Oyster Stew **46**

MAIN DISHES
Baked Stuffed Pike **47**
Lasagne **47**
Bodega Shrimp au Gratin **49**
Roasted Capons with Oyster & Rice Stuffing **49**
Brandy-Buttered Roast Turkey **50**
Herb-Crusted Prime Rib with Port Wine Sauce **50**
Liver & Veal Loaf **50**

RECIPE INDEX

VEGETABLES & SIDE DISHES
Sausage Bread Stuffing 53
Oyster Dressing 53
Cranberry Sauce with Port & Tangerine 53
Double Baked Roquefort Potatoes 53
Old-Fashioned Corn Relish 54
Sweet Potato Fries 54

BREAD, PASTRY, DESSERTS
Creamy Rice Pudding 54
Angel Erdman's Ribbon Gelatin 54
Bananas Foster Shortcake 55
Elaine's Pie Crust 55
Grand Marnier Baked Custard 55
VIP Pecan Pie 56
Sanders Refrigerator Rolls 56
Sanders Coffee Cake & Streusel Topping 56
Sanders Butter Frosting 57
Sanders Glossy Chocolate Fudge Icing 57
Sanders Hot Fudge Topping 57

1980-1992
THE DUNN DRIVE YEARS

APPETIZERS & SOUPS
Artichoke Dip 66
Smoked Whitefish Dip 66
Lavash Cracker Bread 66
Smoked Whitefish Cheesecake 67
Lobster Bisque 67
Country Style Italian Winter Soup 69

MAIN DISHES
Seared Bourbon Street Steaks 69
Golden Garlic Mustard Sauce 69
Pan Seared Filet Mignon with Roasted
  Potatoes 69
Merlot Sauce 70
Strip Steak or Tenderloin 70
Sticky Spicy Ribs 70
Savory Meatloaf 71
Broiled Marinated Chuck Steak 71
Roast Duck with Cherry Wine Sauce 72

FISH DISHES
Steamed Mussels 72
Shrimp Risotto with Orange and Grand
  Marnier 72
Cold Poached Salmon with Mustard
  Lime Sauce 75
Quick Nutty Salmon 75
Steamed Salmon 75
Blackened Fish 75
Crab Cakes 76

SAUCES
Creamy Horseradish Dressing 76
Horseradish Mayonnaise 76
Sour Cream and Horseradish 76
Lemon-Butter Sauce 77
Creole Sauce 77
Pesto 77
Sweet-Sour Sauce 77
20 Minute Spaghetti Sauce 78
Balsamic Vinaigrette 78
Mediterranean Onion Relish 78

SIDE DISHES
Bread & Butter Pickles 78

DESSERTS
Lindsey's Pie Crust 79
Perfect Nut Crust 79
Cheesecake Brulee 79
Lacy Dessert Baskets 79
Cannoli 80
Orleans Apple Torte 80
Mountain-High Key Lime Pie 81
Marie-Chantal's Keyboard
  Birthday Cake 81

RECIPE INDEX

1993-2006
CHATEAU CHANTAL

BREAKFAST MAIN DISHES
Cheese Soufflé Roll w/Spinach Filling 90
Breakfast Pizza 90
Angel Puffs 91
Eggs Mornay with Fresh Tomato Sauce 91
Eggs Florentine with Asiago Cheese 91
Crustless Vegetable Quiche 92
Ham and Cheese Frittata 92
Eggs Benedict and Creamy Hollandaise
  Sauce 92
Geraldine's Basic Crepes 92
Pannakuku 93
Eggs-Artichoke Sausage Casserole 93
Cherry Cheese Strata 93
Creamed Eggs 94
Poached Eggs Chardonnay 94
Shrimp and Scrambled Eggs 94
Spinach Stuffed Portabello Mushrooms 97
Tomatoes Rockefeller 97

MUFFINS AND QUICK BREADS
Glorious Muffins 97
Artichoke Bread 97
Apricot and Almond Muffins 98
Blueberry Muffins 98
Cranberry-Walnut Streusel Muffins 98
Cinnamon Swirl Bread 99
Raisin Pumpkin Bread 99

WAFFLES AND TOAST
Crispy Waffles 99
Pumpkin Waffles 101
Peach French Toast 101
Very Cherry Stuffed French Toast 101
Raisin Cinnamon Toast 102

COOKIES
Oatmeal Cookies 102
Cherry Garcia Cookies 102
Belgian Molasses Cookies 103
Coconut Macaroon Cookies 103
Coconut Oat Cookies 103

PASTRIES
Cousin Lucille's Banquette 103
Cream Puffs 104
Easy Pecan Rolls 104
Double Cranberry Biscotti 104
Popovers 104
Luscious Apricot Bars 105
Canadian Sugar Pie 105
Polish Country Cheesecake 105
Select Harvest Gewurztraminer Cake 106
Pecan Tarts 106
Fresh Fruit Tarts 106
Almond Cakes 108

SOUP, SALADS, APPETIZERS
Bay Pointe Chowder Soup 108
Shrimp, Zucchini and Red Bell Pepper
  Bisque 109
Oyster and Brie Champagne Soup 109
Warm Goat Cheese Salad 110
Cheese and Wine Spread 110
Bruschetta 114

SIDE DISHES
Roasted Root Vegetables with Apple Juice
  and Wine 110
Sugared Bacon 110
Smoked Whitefish Paté 112
Spinach Stuffed Onion Rings 112
Smoked Trout Cheesecake 112

CANDY
Divinity 115
Caramels 115
Chocolate Caramels 115
Vanilla Caramels 115
Icewine Truffles 116
Cherry Brandy Truffles 116
Chocolate Marquise 116
Pecan Roll 116
Butter Crunch 116
Opera Fudge 117
Peanut Butter Balls 117
Crunchy Nutty Popcorn 117

A DAY HEMMED IN PRAYER IS LESS LIKELY TO UNRAVEL

The fabric of Christ's love has been woven with different textures, intense and tinted colors with many unpredicted designs...my birth in the city, our family days at the farm, my courage to leave it all, becoming a nun, teaching, leaving the convent, saying 'yes' to Robert, holding Marie-Chantal in my heart forever, our travels, the many beautiful homes we had and have, great friends along the way...deeply grateful, **DEO GRATIAS!.** The hundredfold promised by the Lord is here **TODAY** .

The end of my story...the end of the cruise where most of my life story was written…

Today is Pentecost. The vibrant rushing wind is filling the day with energy, warmth and delight and Christ is speaking with power and certitude.

He is here. We have had a marvelous journey from Croatia to Venice to Sicily, Monte Carlo and Barcelona. It has come to a reluctant end. The ocean has been my constant companion revealing the 'mysterious movement of God."

A PENTECOST SEQUIENCE

"Come Spirit who energizes our being

Keep us from the tangles of toil and travail

Lead us to moments of prayer and play"

Joyce Rupp

A FINAL PRAYER

In 1944 Sister Emmanuel had given me a prayer book. One prayer from the book has remained with me to this day...from the stairs in the farmhouse to the convent dormitories, to the mission places, to Detroit, Bay City, our travels to Europe and now to the beautiful Bays of Traverse City…

NIGHT HAS FALLEN…

Night has fallen, dearest Mother, and the long night is o'er
And before thy loving image I am here once more.
To thank thee for keeping me safe during this day
And to ask thee this night to keep evil away.
Many times I have fallen, dear Mother. Many graces neglected since last I
Knelt here.
Will thou not in pity, my own dear Mother mild, ask Jesus to pardon the sins of
His child.
I am going to rest for the day's work is done.
The hours and moments have passed one by one.
The God who will judge me has counted each grace and numbered each fall.
In His book they are written against the last Day.
O, Mother, ask Jesus to wash them away.

For one drop of His blood which for sinners was spilt
Is sufficient to cleanse the whole world from its guilt.
And if e'er the dawn I should draw my last breath
And the sleep that I take be the sleep of death,
Be near me, dear Mother, for Jesus's sake.
When my soul on Eternity's shore shall awake.

Heart talks with Mary

Rosalie Marie Levy, 1944

AMEN !

Sacred Expression
There is an expectant hush,
The baton is raised,
I hear a prelude
Stirring in my soul,
Whispers and murmuring
Quiet, and yet bold.
Allegro, Andante, Adagio,
An all-consuming symphony,
The music of my destiny,
Born of my Creator,
Jesus Christ, my Lord and Savior.
Through prayer and contemplation
I followed His command,
Each string and note and tempo
Held firmly in His hand,
Leading, affirming,
His will for me discerning
Tranquil, flowing melodies,
Perfect, vibrant harmonies
Crescendos, fortes, pianissimos
And minor movements of discord,

When patiently He'd wait with me
Till I as in accord.
In the silence of each rest
His perfect peace I found
To give me strength and comfort
In measures He knows best,
For the works of His Hands
Are faithful and just,
In Jesus Christ I place my life
And my trust.

Earlene McMillan

IN CONCLUSION

It is with humble elation that I express heartfelt gratitude for this beautiful life that I was blessed with and embraced. My wonderful family: Daddy, Mom, Carolyn, Genevieve, Frances, Joseph, Angel, and Mary. So many memorable Christmases and always a new Easter bonnet.

Joe and I were close in age and we became the best of friends. The year Angel spent in the convent sealed our love and friendship. Mary, my youngest sister, became special after inviting two of her children to live with us for two years.

The twenty-two years I spent in the convent were truly beautiful… sad sometimes, but inspiring. I missed my family, especially at Christmas. Jesus and I got to know and love each other.

The first years at the convent, I attended Madonna College, graduated and continued my education at Wayne State University, received an MA, and continued to teach.

My first assignment was in Livonia, Mi. at St. Michael Parish. Following that I was assigned to St. Valentine in Livonia, St Stanislaus in Detroit, and St Florian in Hamtramck. One memory from that assignment I will remember forever. A group of high school seniors was walking behind me. I heard them singing, 'Nadine baby, is that you?" I kept on walking. Now I would have said, "You got it!"

I continued teaching at St Stanislaus in Bay City, MI, a place I truly loved. I taught 50 children how to receive the Lord for the first time. I can still hear my mother saying, "Patty, if you did noting else but teach those children to receive Jesus, that was enough."

The blessings continued to abound after leaving the convent. I knew Rev. Robert Begin from the year that I spent at St. Margaret Mary in Detroit. The Felicians, at that time, allowed an experimental year in the convent. We retained vows And were allowed to wear lay clothes in place of the habit. This gave a bit more freedom to associate more freely with parents, children, and those in the parish.

After the year expired, Reverend Mother called and said, "Either come back, put the habit on, go where we assign you, do what we ask of you, or LEAVE." Having tasted freedom made it impossible to return. So we responded, "Adios, amigos", and our new beginnings of life began.

I learned to drive, bought a Red Duster, taught school at Bishop Foley and rented an apartment in Royal Oak, Mi. It was heavenly to have a taste of freedom for the first time in my life. I truly enjoyed the new experiences.

Several months pass...the telephone rings. Yes, it was Robert. "How would you like a little

Company tonight?" He had begun the process of laicization and no longer would continue in the priesthood. The calls became more frequent.

We were in Canada at the *Ye Ole Steakhouse* when Robert held up his glass of wine and proposed in French. We were married on October 4, 1974. The blessings continued to abound.

In the absence of a pregnancy, we invited Charlie and Beth, my niece and nephew, to live with us. And lo, and behold — a year later Marie-Chantal was born on March 10, 1978. She attended Old Mission Grade School, graduated from high school in Traverse City, then on to degrees at DePaul University Chicago, and winery management at University of Adelaide, Australia.

It was in Aussieland that Marie found the love of her life, Paul Dalese. They married, moved to Traverse City, now have a son named Luca, who is the last intense joy of my life. Jesus has blessed me with a touch of heaven on earth.

I am abundantly blessed with the love of Jesus, Robert, Chantal, Paul and Luca. Praise the Lord! I thank each and every one of you for making my life one of beauty, joy, and love!

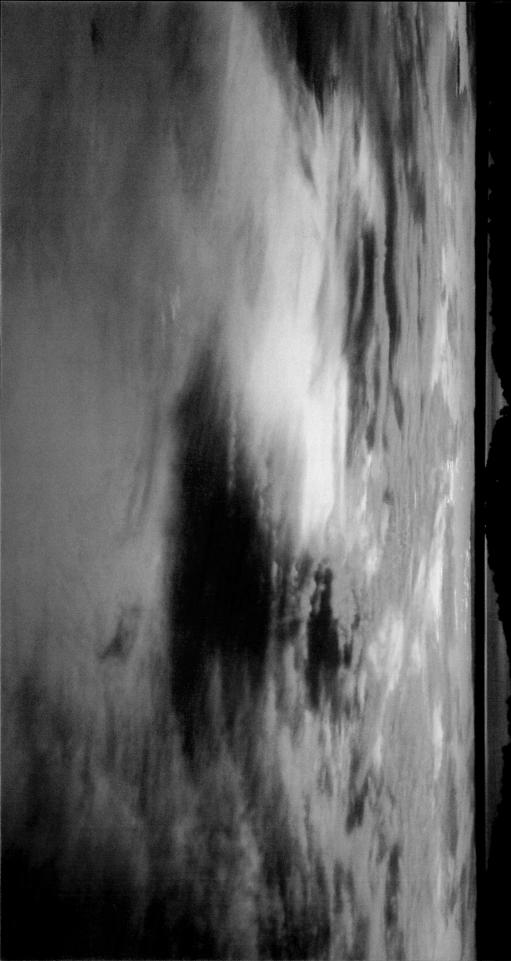

In appreciation

Julianne Wolny
You are the most faitful, perservering and loving friend one could find this side of heaven. The strength of your vision resulted in the reality of *Feed My Lambs, Feed My Sheep*. Over periods of years, you have edited my recipes and stories, bringing a conclusion to this labor of love.

Earlene McMillin
You are my friend and creator of unparalleled, mystifying poetry. With this unique gift, you interpret my innermost stirrings of heart and soul. As you say, "I'm sure that our Beloved Jesus brought us together to enrich not only our lives, but others as well."

Kathleen Debra Ott
Creative Director of Indy Productions—Photography, Photos-scape and Greeting Cards. Your creative presentations are unique, charming and delightful to the eye. Frolicking in your garden and woods has resulted in a refreshing assortment of props.

Susan Kelly Arnold
An artist blessed with abundant talents, overflowing generosity and a beautiful friend.

Paige Billette
Employee at Chateau Chantal, Assistant Food Photographer

Scarlet Piedmont
Wedding Photographer

Marie-Chantal
My beautiful daughter. You have deluged my life with great joy, lots of fun and a wonderful, Australian son-in-law, Paul Dalese.

And thanks to all who have contibuted recipes throughout these many years and to my special friends *(see next pages)*.

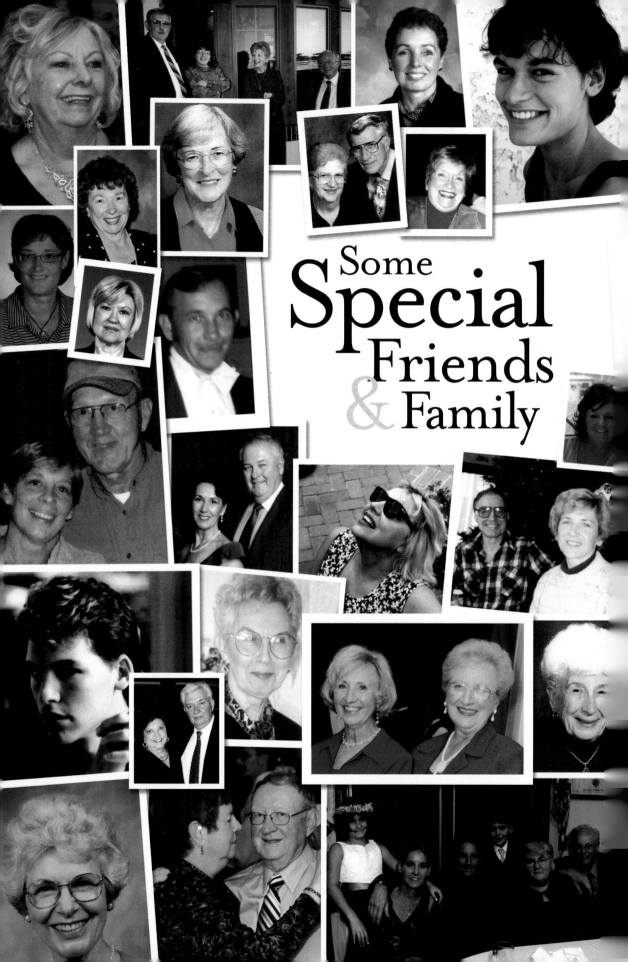

Some
Special
& Friends
Family